NOT HOW I DREW IT UP

One Man's Unthinkable Journey to Fatherhood

MATT SEIGEL

ISBN:
979-8-9938432-0-9 (Paperback)
979-8-9938432-1-6 (Ebook)

For all of my boys, without whom

this book couldn't exist.

Foreword

"Grief is the price we pay for love."

—Queen Elizabeth II

Have you ever attended a funeral for a child? It's one of the most heartbreaking, gut-wrenching experiences you'll ever face. And if it's your own child, well, that's an entirely different level of heartbreak.

This book is based on a real story: my story.

Because losing a son is the greatest tragedy I've faced – and will ever face.

Because every man should know what to expect before, during, and after childbirth when things don't go as planned.

Because there's not a lot of reading material from the male perspective on fertility struggles and infant loss.

Because I hope that by putting my experience on paper, I can help just one person avoid some of the potentially long road to completing their family.

This book doesn't have all the answers, because fertility and childbirth are, as I learned the hard way, an inexact science. What it does contain is a real-world example of just how challenging it can be for a partner to become a parent to the children he and his spouse have been dreaming of since they first began dating. It's my sincere hope that if you're reading this, you recognize two things: first, this book isn't an attempt at a pity party; second, the sum of the hurdles we overcame to complete our family is extraordinarily rare, however not "one in a million." In other words, if you are thinking of having kids, expecting, or anywhere in between, let this serve as a cautionary tale to be an active participant in your fertility journey— nothing is a certainty. There will be twists and turns, roadblocks and setbacks. While it's good to have a plan, it's even better to be prepared to pivot.

Chapter One

After my wife Jenya and I got married, we knew we weren't going to have much time to be "DINKs" (dual income, no kids) because: 1, we both wanted kids and 2, we were both in our mid-30s. So, when Jenya got pregnant one of the first times we tried, we were stoked! We were living in Boston at the time, and she found a doctor she really liked. I'll never forget the sheer joy I felt when she told me. Joy, and then "Yikes!!!" Can I do this? Will I be ready to be a dad in eight months? Can we truly afford to be raising another human being?

A few weeks later, it was time for our first ultrasound. When mom is considered high-risk (which my wife was because of her age), this ultrasound typically happens around 6-8 weeks into a pregnancy. Jenya's doctor happened to have an office inside one of the larger hospitals in Boston, which was conveniently located close to our apartment. Prior to this appointment, I could count on one hand the number of times I'd been inside a hospital. I'm fortunate to be pretty healthy, with two broken bones in my life and no major ailments requiring a trip to the hospital.

So, we went in for our ultrasound, Jenya got on the table, and an ultrasound technician began the process of inserting a wand into her vagina. I was focused on a monitor that, if you've never seen one before, you might describe as a radar screen looking at outer space. In other words, I had absolutely no clue what we were looking at, other than that we were looking for a heartbeat on a tiny embryo. And if you've never seen a six-week ultrasound, the best way to describe that heartbeat would be nothing more than a twinkling star on the screen. But of course they didn't tell me, the father, what we were looking for, ahead of time…at least not in Boston. A minute or so went by and the tech said to us, "Let me go get the doctor. I'll be back in just a minute." Jenya squeezed my arm and started crying uncontrollably. I was completely caught off guard as to why she was so upset. "I knew it, it's a miscarriage!" she exclaimed while bawling her eyes out. MISCARRIAGE? I had absolutely no clue how this could be possible. "She just peed on a pregnancy test the other day and the lines were so dark," I thought. As you continue to read, you'll see this is the first of many instances where my mindset and my wife's were completely different because we were experiencing the same thing in very different ways.

A doctor who we'd never met came into the room and re-inserted the probe. She was manipulating the probe to look at my wife's uterus and stopped when she saw a lifeless embryo. "There is the baby," she said. "And I'm very sorry to tell you that there is no heartbeat."

Jenya was crying and now I was right there with her. I knew miscarriages were a thing, but until this happened, I had no idea how often they occurred. According to the March of Dimes, between 10-20% of known pregnancies end in miscarriage[1]. Anecdotally, I've heard that the rate might be even higher. The doctor explained to us that there were a couple of choices we had as a next step because my wife needed to pass the embryonic tissue out of her body: there was some medication she could take that would accelerate a post-pregnancy bleed, or there was a surgical procedure that could be done. My wife, not wanting to increase the mental trauma that might come with a heavy bleed at home, opted for the latter, called a dilation and curettage, or D&C.

The D&C was scheduled for the next day. We returned to the hospital and the doctor explained that Jenya would be put under anesthesia for the procedure, which should take about 10-15 minutes. They wheeled her back into a procedure room while I stayed in a waiting room. This was the first time I was alone in a hospital, waiting for someone to have a procedure. It was fine at

---

1. https://www.marchofdimes.org/find-support/topics/miscarriage-loss-grief/miscarriage

first, but then my mind started going places. 15 minutes went by. Then 20. Then 30. I was starting to get a little concerned. Then, about 40 minutes after Jenya was wheeled away, her doctor came out and said to me, "Matt, we weren't able to do the D&C." It's been about ten years since this happened, but I'm fairly certain I said something to the effect of, "Well then what the hell happened back there?" The doctor explained that Jenya's cervix wasn't cooperating (i.e., dilating) with the instruments they had and that we'd have to do this another day, after they gave her additional medication to soften her cervix (and get thinner instruments to do the job). They also explained that it was possible that my wife hadn't miscarried and that the dates of the pregnancy were off and maybe we would see a heartbeat if we waited a bit. We were asked to return after a week and recheck for a heartbeat. If we didn't see the heartbeat then, we would retry the D&C with the additional medication. In a matter of 48 hours we'd had a miscarriage, a failed D&C, and I was now dealing with a wife who was emotionally spent (as was I). And…we had to wait a week to see if we had actually miscarried.

It was a long, stressful week in a cold, snowy winter. We'd go to work, try to do our best, come home, and try to be kind to each other. It wasn't easy but we knew we had to trudge through those next few days. When we went back to the hospital a week later, our suspicion was confirmed; there was no heartbeat, and we needed to proceed with the D&C. In true Boston form, it was an absolute blizzard outside, so I decided to leave our car with the valet at the hospital. We went back to the same area we were at the previous week, they wheeled her away, and 15 minutes later the doctor came out and said, "Success. Jenya will be groggy from the anesthesia, but you two will be able to go home in about an hour. I'm so sorry for all of this hassle." I was able to walk to a recovery room and hug my wife after the first "successful" (and I use that term VERY loosely) procedure. I felt a sense of relief that she was OK and that we had some closure to this traumatic experience. A nurse suggested I go give our valet ticket to someone and that she would wheel Jenya down shortly. I followed her instructions, headed downstairs, and Jenya was wheeled down about 10 minutes later. We waited about 45 minutes as the continuing snowstorm snarled any semblance of traffic to a halt. But that wait paled in comparison to what we would wait even longer for…a healthy child.

March of Dimes uses 15% as an average miscarriage rate, however doctors we've interacted with say it's even higher – more in the 25-30% range. If it happens to you and your partner, you're hardly alone.

If your partner is considered 'high risk,' don't hesitate to ask for ultrasounds earlier than normal. You and your partner should be advocating for the baby from day one – and nobody else will advocate as strongly as you two.

It's perfectly okay to ask the OB/doctor/tech ahead of time what you can expect to see on an ultrasound monitor. Sometimes professionals assume that people already know certain things, but there is a lot of new information you will be absorbing, so it's okay to ask.

Early transvaginal ultrasounds can be performed without the audio if you choose. This can minimize any potential heat effects from the acoustic output of a Doppler ultrasound.[2] As exciting as it might be to hear the heartbeat, visual confirmation is all you need early in a pregnancy.

---

2. https://www.aium.org/resources/official-statements/view/prudent-use-and-safety-of-diagnostic-ultrasound-in-pregnancy

Chapter Two

There are multiple published studies that report the chances of a successful pregnancy increase if you are able to get pregnant within the first three months following a miscarriage as opposed to waiting longer. Armed with that information, along with our ages (late 30s) and our "want to," we were ready to get back on that horse! After Jenya got a period, we tried over a fcw months, but nothing stuck. Shortly thereafter, our careers brought us back to the Midwest. As soon as we settled in, we were referred to a local fertility doctor. At the time, there were only a couple of options within a half hour of our new house and the physician we went to had a decent reputation.

Our first appointment with this doctor was memorable - probably because we sat in her office for over an hour, waiting for her to arrive. We were told she was tied up with a procedure in the adjacent hospital. But after her grand entrance, she walked us through the in-vitro fertilization (IVF) process and gave my inquisitive wife all the answers she was looking for, while doing her best to pretend I wasn't even in the room. Yes, in that 30–40-minute appointment, I'm fairly certain the doctor looked at me no more than twice. Get used to it, partners…we are NOT the patient; we're basically the supporting actors. Despite the delay, we left with a general consensus that she would be a suitable provider for us.

If you're unfamiliar with IVF, here's the gist: the female partner injects a cocktail of hormones into her body at specific times during her ovulation cycle to stimulate her ovaries to produce many eggs. Some younger women will produce 10-20 eggs that are then surgically retrieved at the end of the cycle. Meanwhile, the male partner (or sperm donor, if needed) produces a semen sample (read: you masturbate in the doctor's office) which is then combined with the eggs to produce as many embryos as possible. It's a total numbers game; I've heard of some cycles resulting in 18+ embryos, and others end up with none.

There is a simpler, less expensive option called intrauterine insemination (IUI), which involves placing sperm directly into a woman's uterus around the time of ovulation to improve the chances of fertilization. This is sometimes referred to as the "turkey baster" method. It's less invasive than IVF, but generally less successful, especially for couples with more complex fertility issues. Regardless of outcome with either method, you're on the hook financially or through insurance for all of this.

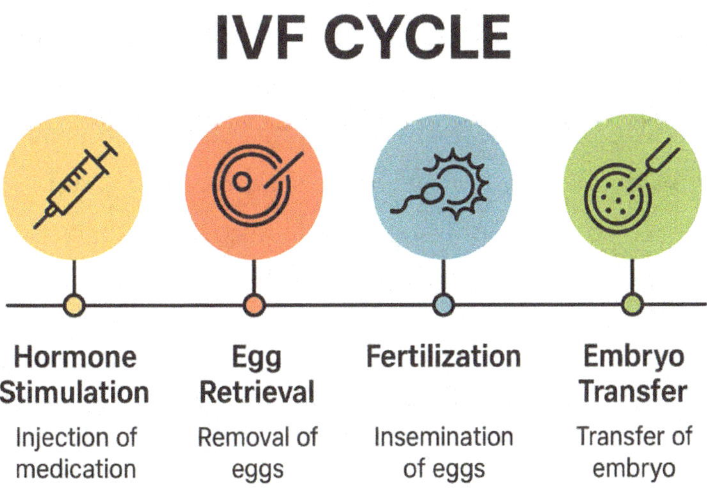

Our first IVF cycle began with Jenya having to inject herself in the thigh each night for a few weeks. She was also going back and forth to the doctor's office throughout the cycle so they could monitor her progress using ultrasounds. They checked how the follicles (eggs) were growing and sometimes adjusted her medication based on this. As you'd expect, the synthetic hormones Jenya was adding to her body caused her emotions to significantly fluctuate. Of course, I wanted to support her however I could; but partners reading this, know that this isn't one of those things you will be able to fix. If you go down this road, be prepared for a calm and composed wife one moment—and an entirely different experience the next. And if you're a woman reading this, know that the emotional rollercoaster you are on is perfectly normal.

Right before it was time for the egg retrieval, we would inject HCG (i.e., the pregnancy hormone) as a trigger shot. Keep in mind that these shots are supposed to all be done at roughly the same time each night. If you're home, great. If you're not home, you are doing these injections wherever. Have you ever hooked up with someone in your car, or the bathroom of a restaurant, because that was your only option? Consider this part of your journey "the hookup" – a far less sexy hookup.

On the day of the egg retrieval, we went to the hospital adjacent to the doctor's office for the procedure. This was done under sedation and can cause mild to moderate discomfort. They wheeled her away to the operating room, I waited (with images of our Boston experience floating in my head) and a half hour or so later, the doctor came out. "We retrieved six eggs," she told me. "Jenya did great." They'd combine the eggs with my sperm, and we'd find out a few days later how many eggs were fertilized. Even though that number of eggs felt like a good amount to me, the wait was still agonizing for both of us.

Three days later, we got the call. Four embryos! We were elated, knowing that we had a pretty decent shot one of them would be "the one." IVF clinics assign letter grades to each embryo – in theory, a higher-graded embryo has a greater chance to develop into a fetus, and ultimately a newborn. However, many doctors will tell you that the grading isn't a perfect indicator of success.

A few weeks after the retrieval came the transfer. Imagine a plastic siphoning tube, only as thin as one of those glass thermometers you stick under your tongue. The doctor extracts an embryo and fluid from a petri dish and carefully inserts the catheter (that thin tube) into the woman's uterus. Voila! Now comes the fun part…the two-week wait to see if she's pregnant. For some women, this means patiently waiting a couple weeks until it's time to return to the doctor's office for a pregnancy blood test. For the vast majority of women I've discussed this with, it involves stocking up on an endless supply of at-home pregnancy tests so that she can pee on a stick on a daily basis (or more likely, multiple times per day) to see if she's actually pregnant. I found it to be quite obsessive, but I wasn't the one full of hormones. For what it's worth, the cheap paper strip pregnancy tests work as well as the expensive drugstore ones and my wife was getting Amazon deliveries with boxes of 25-50 strips each cycle. If you recall, she had taken an HCG trigger shot, which causes a positive pregnancy test until it is fully out of your body. My wife was testing each day to see the positive line fade from the trigger shot. Once it was finally negative (after about 2 weeks), she hoped for a positive line to show again meaning she was actually pregnant. For us, we weren't so fortunate on the first try – Jenya had what's called a chemical pregnancy. This is essentially a positive pregnancy test, followed by a miscarriage shortly thereafter – within the first five weeks of pregnancy.

Despite having three additional embryos in the freezer, we decided to do another egg retrieval at the recommendation of the doctor due to my wife's "advanced maternal age." Egg quality diminishes as women get older, and we wanted to harvest more eggs in case we needed them to complete our family. The next cycle only yielded three eggs; none of which fertilized into a viable embryo. This was obviously disappointing for both of us. For my wife, there were many times when she felt like she wasn't doing her job well enough. Of course, this was hardly the case – she was in her late 30s, and the treatment just wasn't stimulating her ovaries well enough. I tried to provide Jenya with the reassurance that she *was* doing all the right things in the right way to help us grow our family. Personally, it was frustrating to spend so much time and energy with no positive result. It felt like time wasted when she could have been pregnant with one of the other embryos we had from the first cycle. It didn't feel logical to me, but I was putting my faith into the expertise of the doctor and yielding to Jenya's ultimate wishes – her body, her choice.

We attempted one more transfer with one of the embryos from the first cycle, and that embryo didn't grow. In other words, we were two rounds of IVF in, with two transfers, and nothing to show for it, other than a lot of time and a large chunk of change spent. We were tired, frustrated, and wondered if we were doing the right thing. We have friends who've had children via IVF, so we know it works, but we kept asking ourselves, why not us? These miscarriages were so devastating for both of us; however, the grief process is quite different for men and women. For a man or non-carrying partner, it's quite possible that he or she will be sad, upset, frustrated, or confused for several days. But typically, those emotions will regulate sooner than those of a pregnant partner, which is to be expected. Women literally have pregnancy hormones in their body, and no baby to show for it. As her hormone levels returned to baseline (which could be a 6-8-week process), Jenya's mood was unstable, and that was exceptionally trying for me. There were many moments when we could've quit trying to have kids, or even split up. The stress and continuous feeling of defeat was excruciating for us both. But that wasn't Jenya, nor was it me. We had to move forward, and we were starting to feel desperate; it was time to get a second opinion from another doctor.

IVF protocols can differ among doctors; if geographically feasible for you, it would be worth your time to interview more than one doctor and compare their success rates. You might be surprised how much they can vary.

Despite the "grades" given to embryos, a better grade is not always indicative of a greater likelihood of a successful pregnancy. Experienced physicians include numerous factors to recommend the "best" embryo for transfer and sometime recommend testing of the embryos.

Expect your wife/partner to be riding a roller coaster of emotions during an IVF cycle; the synthetic hormones she is being injected with unquestionably affect a woman's psyche;

some men say their spouse turned into "a different person" while she was going through IVF.

In the moment, a miscarriage is going to feel awful for both partners. You will cope differently, and it is best to cut each other lots of slack as you process this grief differently.

Chapter Three

After two cycles with the same doctor, limited frozen embryos, and our patience wearing thin, we decided it was time to explore a different fertility center a little farther from our house. The Society for Assisted Reproductive Technology (SART) is the non-profit organization that is the standard bearer for infertility treatment. One of the best parts of the organization and its website, SART.org, is its free outcomes reporting. You can compare the IVF success rates of any member clinic to the national average or to another clinic. The vast majority of reputable clinics are members and will gladly refer you to this information as you do your research.

The new clinic we selected had multiple locations in Chicagoland – all they do is help couples build their families. We knew people who used this doctor and clinic, and we were excited at the prospect of finding something that actually worked. Our first meeting with the doctor went better than our first meeting with the previous doctor. First, he was punctual! Second, he carefully explained his protocol for medication, and it was much more aggressive and involved than our previous experience. Third, he was audacious enough to tell us that our previous doctor, while an excellent endocrinologist and surgeon, doesn't do nearly as many IVF transfers as his clinic. He told us he essentially ran an IVF factory, so he knew exactly how to properly stimulate the ovaries to produce a large quantity of eggs. And he had the numbers to back it up. We were sold (not that it was a sales pitch – it wasn't).

Step one of the IVF cycle at this clinic was a hysteroscopy under sedation. This is done to check the uterus for any scar tissue, polyps, or anything else that might prohibit a successful embryo transfer. Unfortunately, in many cases, it requires anesthesia – which means a half day off work for you (assuming you are joining your wife for this procedure) and your partner. And let's be clear: there is going to be a lot of time taken off work to attend appointments throughout any pregnancy journey. Because of the volume of patients at this clinic, they usually schedule procedures requiring anesthesia early in the morning and embryo transfers and other appointments that don't require an anesthesiologist later in the day. Since the clinic was an hour away, that meant an early wake up call for our 7am appointment. In what might be one of my fondest memories of this entire process, I knew the anesthesiologist was already in the building because the luxury car we parked next to had a license plate that said *IGASEM*! The back entrance to the office, which is where we would go for all of our procedures, was unique in that there was a small waiting area with just 3-4 chairs and a doorbell. A nurse would come to the door and escort patients into the facility. I was amazed; 20 feet past the door, there were six patient "rooms" that were separated by nothing more than some heavy curtains. It was hardly soundproof, but private enough. I'll refer to this area as the "holding pen," as it was essentially an area where the nurses wheeled patients into the operating room down the hallway. Each "room" had a gurney, a couple of chairs, and an end table. There were a couple of dimmable ceiling can lights – these spaces could get quite dark if you wanted to rest. We could hear the doctors and nurses speaking with other patients, albeit softly. This was an IVF factory if there ever was one! The hysteroscopy was relatively routine; a small polyp was removed, Jenya recovered nicely from the sedation, we were given discharge instructions and prescriptions to fill, and we were on our way.

For this round of IVF, a cocktail of hormones was prescribed for Jenya. One of the shots was to be injected into her thigh, but the other was to go into her glute. And just like that, I was called to duty. Forget sex: I was going to be poking my wife in the rear with a syringe on a nightly basis for the next several weeks. Bear in mind, I've never been a fan of needles – I usually turn away when I get blood drawn. This wasn't going to be easy for either of us. The first night, we watched a video to ensure that I would hit the right spot (basically, in line with the top of the butt crack on the outer half of the cheek). Jenya gets all the credit for this next idea: I would draw a circle on her body with a sharpie so she could approve of the location before I stuck her. Then, an at-home medical process I quickly became an expert at performing: Rub an alcohol wipe over the injection area, connect a needle to the syringe, insert it into the vial of medication and draw up the prescribed amount, switch the needle off the syringe to a different one with a fresh, sharp point, and BAM! In went the hormones, out came a "why'd you do that!" "You told me to!" Welcome to varsity level IVF.

The nightly injections continued for a couple of weeks. My wife's derriere was black and blue from all of the poking. There were some nights when she found the injections to be more painful than others. I was doing my best, but we agreed that this was not pleasant for either of us. Jenya had to have bloodwork done on a weekly basis to see where her hormone levels were, as the doctor would adjust medication levels in real time if things weren't progressing as they should. There were also some ultrasounds that allowed the doctor to measure the size of the follicles each ovary was producing; once they got to a target size, the egg retrieval was scheduled. One last shot – the hCG trigger shot – was administered 36 hours before the retrieval. A day and a half later, it was another early wakeup call for a trip to the clinic. Just like at our first doctor's office, the retrieval was a fairly invasive, somewhat uncomfortable procedure done under sedation. This time around, they retrieved seven eggs. I subsequently provided my semen sample the same day and we waited three days to see how many eggs were fertilized.

We got the call – five of the seven eggs fertilized! We also elected to do PGS (preimplantation genetic screening) testing on these embryos. This allows doctors to determine viability of each embryo and transfer the one(s) most likely to lead to a successful pregnancy. The only downside is it means the fresh embryos have to be frozen, and then thawed, before transfer. There is some risk to the embryo in doing this, but a frozen transfer is quite standard in the IVF world. In some cases, it seems that frozen embryos are more successful in achieving pregnancy.

We got the results from the PGS testing; only one was viable, and we'd be transferring that embryo the following week. We made another trip to the clinic (this one for a 10am appointment – no early wakeup call!) and had a brief wait in the holding pen. Then, two nurses came to wheel Jenya away and one of them said to me, "You're coming with, right?" Wait a minute…I get to be a part of this? Who knew! This was probably the first time throughout our entire journey that I actually felt like an equal in this process. I walked in behind Jenya into a procedure room that felt like a sauna. It turns out the temperature needs to stay warm for the embryo's health. There were three or four nurses and assistants in the room; Jenya was situated in the middle with some bright surgical lights pointed at the lower half of her body. They had a chair for me right next to Jenya. A couple of large flat screen televisions were on the walls. There was a door to another room – I was told the lab was on the other side of the door, which was split in half so they could open just part of it when needed. Even though she was the one about to have an embryo implanted into her, I also felt like the center of attention. It was exciting and nerve-wracking, but it felt like we were making some serious progress at this clinic.

After we signed some consent forms and verified we were transferring one embryo (more on this later), the doctor walked in. This doctor was the partner of the physician we'd been seeing at this clinic, as our main guy just happened to be on vacation the week of our transfer. But we really liked today's doctor; she was kind and seemed to have a terrific bedside manner. She arranged some equipment and inserted a speculum into Jenya's vagina. If you've never seen a speculum before, imagine a caulk gun with a narrow tube of caulk attached…that's the part that goes inside of a woman. Once everything was set, they turned on the TV screen, and we immediately saw a sterile petri dish with our names next to it. Someone behind the lab door inserted some plastic catheter tubing into the dish and sucked up what was inside. Then, the door opened and the lab technician announced to the room, "Jenya and Matthew Seigel, one embryo for transfer." The TV screen then switched to an image of the ultrasound machine that was currently on Jenya's abdomen. The doctor took the catheter, inserted it into the speculum, and slowly released the embryo into Jenya's uterus. I was literally seeing the embryo transfer in real time! Then, the catheter and speculum were removed, and Jenya was wheeled back to our holding room where she was instructed to relax and stay laying down for an hour or so. To alleviate the stress, she had me play some comedic videos on my phone. (If you've never seen a Jimmy Fallon and the Ragtime Gals bit from his show, we highly recommend it!) There was also a study done in 2011 (cited in the medical journal *Fertility and Sterility)* that found a visit from a "medical clown" after an embryo transfer increased success rates to 36% compared to 20% for the women without the comedy show[1]. Is laughter truly the best medicine? We weren't going to leave it to chance! Did I go over my monthly data cap on our phone to play an hour's worth of videos – sure did. (This was before unlimited data plans on cell phones…and the clinic didn't have public Wi-Fi at the time.) These are the things you do when you are grasping at straws – and they are totally OK!

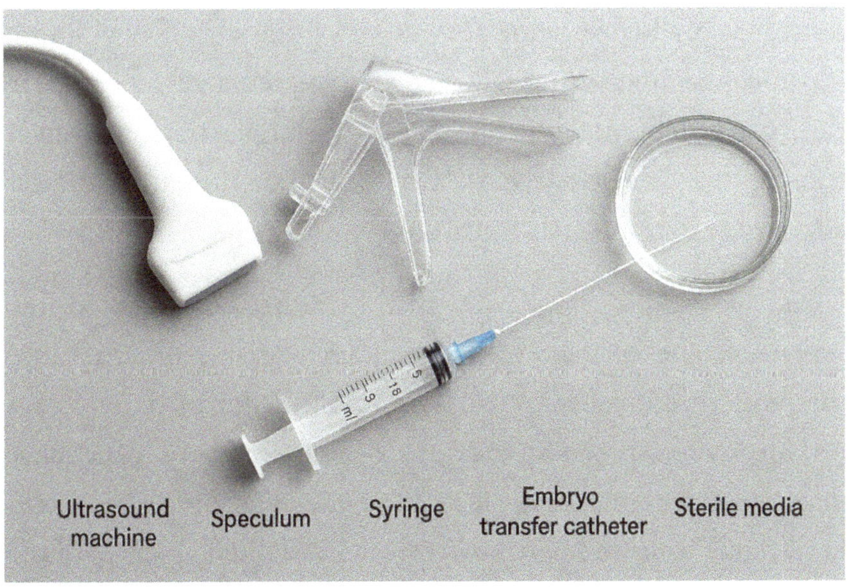

As I mentioned earlier, the instructions from the doctor were

---

1. https://www.fertstert.org/article/S0015-0282(10)02958-4/fulltext

straightforward: no hot tubs, baths, intercourse, or high-impact sports until the first blood test, which comes about 10-14 days after the transfer. But do you really think an anxious, potentially pregnant woman is going to wait that long to learn if she's pregnant? Above our bathroom toilet was a box of pregnancy tests, and Jenya wasted little time breaking into the package, hoping to see two lines (a positive test). She was sometimes taking multiple tests each day. She brought tests to work. She would sit in the bathroom after dinner while I did the dishes. She was texting, chatting, and updating all of her girlfriends, and she was being given hope – lots of hope – by the color of the lines on these sticks and the numbers provided by the blood tests. It was all-consuming for her and from what I now know, it's all-consuming for most women. If you are a partner reading this, you might not be able to relate. But if you're a woman reading this, know that your laser focus over this singular facet of your life is completely normal.

I had no relationship with this hypothetical baby, so my experience and desires were quite different than Jenya's. I'm not the most emotional man you'll meet, and I don't get my hopes up for much, probably because I don't want to experience disappointment – perhaps it's one of my character flaws. I told her I didn't want to know until it was a certainty, so she kept the test results to herself. I think she was annoyed I didn't want to know right along with her, but she respected my choice and was able to connect with plenty of female confidants while I waited for some more formal news. A week later, she went in for bloodwork, where they checked the hCG level…it confirmed a pregnancy! Next, she had to return for more blood work after a few days to determine if the HCG was rising—it is supposed to double every two days or so. With each appointment, it was climbing! This was the kind of news I could celebrate, and so we did. There was a lot more smiling, laughing, and connection with this good news. We had newfound hope, and it was a great feeling for both of us.

Our ultrasound was scheduled right around week six – another drive down to the clinic, and a short wait in the fancy waiting room in the front of the office – not the holding pen where you wait for procedures. We were welcomed into an exam room with a table for Jenya to lay on, a chair for me, and an ultrasound machine on wheels. To say this was a bit nerve-wracking would be an understatement, considering our history with ultrasounds. The doctor walked in, asked how we were doing, and said, "let's take a look." Within a matter of seconds, we saw what appeared to be a flashing star inside Jenya's abdomen…a heartbeat! We're going to have a baby! I gave Jenya a kiss and a hug, a couple of nurses congratulated us, and the doctor told us he'd keep her on hormones through week 12, but for all intents and purposes, we were discharged to our OB back home.

The website sart.org is where the vast majority of IVF clinics post their success rates and is a tremendous resource to help you compare clinics

As an IVF patient, you don't have much of a say when you have an appointment – they tell you when to come, and that's what you do. The laws of supply and demand dictate a lot of this, and there are a LOT of women, men, and couples trying to build a family.

A hysteroscopy under sedation may be performed after failed IVF attempts to inspect the uterus for scar tissue, polyps, or abnormalities that could interfere with implantation.

PGS Testing (Preimplantation Genetic Screening) is used to assess embryos for chromosomal normality; embryos must be frozen after biopsy and thawed before transfer, introducing a small risk but commonly done.

A fetal heartbeat can usually be detected by ultrasound around 6 weeks gestation, confirming a viable early pregnancy. After that confirmation, your time at the IVF clinic is typically complete unless additional medication is needed to ensure a successful pregnancy.

Chapter Four

Jenya and I are fortunate to have a wonderful network of friends in our adopted hometown, and the women are always talking, texting, and conversing about everything and anything pertaining to motherhood. So, it was pretty easy to find a couple of quality referrals for an obstetrician. Picking an OB is similar to picking any other doctor, except for the fact that you're placing trust in this person to care for two people at the same time: the mom and the baby in-utero. I encouraged Jenya to connect with any of the doctors for whom we'd received a positive referral, and she set up an appointment for us with a physician at a nearby OB practice. This practice happened to be located adjacent to the hospital at which we intended to deliver. We went to an initial appointment one afternoon and were greeted by a waiting room with a handful of other expectant mothers, some of whom were accompanied by husbands, some by other women, and a few were there by themselves. I wondered just how many appointments I'd be coming to; Jenya was understandably anxious at this point and really wanted me to attend as many as possible. Considering our track record up to this point, it made perfect sense that she wanted me by her side. That said, I'd be lying if I told you I was truly interested in taking time off work to go to every single appointment. But that's what good partners do, and I was determined to be the best possible husband to the woman I loved the most.

We were led into an exam room and the doctor walked in shortly thereafter. She was friendly and low-key. She answered all of our questions and walked us through a rough plan of how things would go over the next several months. We asked several questions about future appointments, about how far along we would let Jenya stay pregnant before inducing labor, and about what types of resources were available at the delivery hospital. Our doctor was very direct and clear in that first meeting. "You don't need to worry unless I'm worried," she said. That gave us both some peace of mind and a feeling as though we were in good hands. We left that first appointment with a folder of materials including a pamphlet about the hospital's birth center and a "birth preference guide" that we were instructed to fill out. We were encouraged to schedule a tour to see the space where we'd be welcoming our baby into the world. After leaving the office, we gave each other the "nod of approval." If Jenya was good with this doctor, so was I.

One of the questions we asked both our doctor and the hospital was what kind of resources would be available if there was a complication during the delivery. The birth center at the hospital had a Level II NICU (neonatal intensive care unit), also known as a "special care nursery;" according to our doctor, it had everything you'd need except for a ventilator. The sister hospital downtown had a Level III NICU, which is required when babies need more complicated care, on-site neonatologists, and respiratory support. In Wisconsin, there are four levels of NICUs, however Level III is where nearly all babies go when they are born pre-term or needing that respiratory/cardiac support. Level IV NICUs are few and far between; these are major medical centers including the Children's Hospital you may have in your region. Jenya was wise to ask our doctor how often a baby needs the NICU. She told us that they almost always know when that will be the case, and that in all of her time practicing at this hospital, they've only had to transfer one or two babies to the hospital with the Level III NICU.

Because of Jenya's "advanced maternal" age (older than 35), she would have a few more ultrasounds than a younger woman might experience over the course of a pregnancy. At each ultrasound, the baby was measuring appropriately, his heart was beating at the right pace, and all was looking normal. At 20 weeks gestation, there is a more intense anatomy scan, using higher-tech equipment. They measure each limb, count fingers and toes, measure organs – and in many facilities, this is where they can print you one of those 3D pictures of your baby that makes him or her look a little bit like an alien! Still, it's a nice reminder that we had reached the midway point of the pregnancy. In addition to all of these clinical tests, we also elected to do genetic testing to look for any chromosomal abnormalities that could affect the baby. Some parents want to know ahead of time if their baby might have Down syndrome, an abnormal number of X or Y chromosomes, or other potential birth defects. Many of these tests are simple blood tests performed on the mother and can provide peace of mind to parents and medical providers. There is also diagnostic testing called amniocentesis, in which the doctor inserts a thin needle into the uterus to remove a sample of amniotic fluid. We elected to stick to the blood testing, and fortunately everything came back normal for our baby. It was on to the back half of the second trimester.

As Jenya's pregnancy evolved, so did her emotions. While totally normal for an expectant mother, this can catch many partners off guard: it could be sunshine and roses one minute and a torrential thunderstorm the next! I received sound advice from many other partners worth sharing here: remember that it's only temporary, because once that baby comes out, her focus is going to be on the needs of the little one. Do what you can to keep her happy and get out of the way when you feel like you should. For my wife, happiness involved me running to the local Dairy Queen to order a chocolate Blizzard with chocolate candy shell blended in. And Reese's peanut butter cups. Let's just say that by the third time I walked into the store…at 8:30pm in the dead of winter…the owner knew my name and my order. She also asked if my wife knew about gestational diabetes!

By the start of the third trimester, we were having doctor's visits every 2-3 weeks. While many were brief, they were good status checks for both of us. We also began a 4-week series of prenatal classes. There are a variety of classes out there, from how to put on a diaper and swaddle to singing to your baby and massaging their back. I was mainly concerned with safety issues, so we took an infant CPR class and learned how to perform a Heimlich maneuver (also known as back blows) on an infant, among other things. It was nice to see that we weren't the only ones who felt compelled to take such a class; there were other first-time parents in the group, as well as parents with kids who simply wanted a refresher. It was good bonding time for us, plus we could stop for ice cream on the way home.

In the final month of pregnancy, Jenya started having weekly NSTs, or non-stress tests. This entailed a 30-minute visit to the delivery hospital where she would be connected to doppler sonography to check the baby's heart rate. They would also perform a vaginal exam to see if there was any dilation. Despite her not dilating, our doctor expressed no concern as it simply appeared as though we'd have an induction right around the due date. Of course, just because the doctor says it doesn't mean my wife isn't going to feel it! The anticipation, excitement, and anxiety were ever-present in our house over the final weeks leading up to our due date. The plan was now set: it was very unlikely she would be going into labor on her own and we'd be heading to the hospital for an induction two nights before the baby's actual due date. Our OB explained to us that we'd arrive in the evening, and it would be a relatively slow induction; we'd likely have a baby in our arms 12-16 hours after we arrived. If only that were the case...

It's so important to thoroughly vet both the OB and the hospital in which you plan to deliver. Ask questions about contingency plans (is there a NICU, what happens if the baby needs special care, etc.) You can never ask too many questions before committing to an obstetrician.

Due to advanced maternal age (over 35), the pregnancy included additional ultrasounds, a detailed 20-week anatomy scan, and genetic blood testing for chromosomal abnormalities (e.g., Down syndrome), all of which returned normal results. Again, most of these tests are routine for all pregnancies, but are especially meaningful if you've struggled to get pregnant.

In the final trimester, routine non-stress tests (NSTs) were performed weekly to monitor fetal heart rate, and vaginal exams checked for cervical dilation as labor approached.

With no spontaneous labor progression, the OB scheduled a slow labor induction to begin two nights before the due date, anticipating delivery within 12 - 16 hours. Inductions are also routine if mom's cervix isn't dilating on its own.

Chapter Five

We arrived at the hospital for an induction on a crisp winter Wednesday night – February 1, 2017. The hospital was about 10 minutes from our house, and we'd been on a tour of the entire facility, so there were no surprises when we arrived. One of the "features" of this hospital was that the "suite style" rooms are all-in-one; that is, a woman goes through Labor, Delivery, Recovery, and Postpartum in the same room. The hospital also marketed itself as having "hotel-like bathrooms" and amenities, along with rollaway beds for the husband/partner. We didn't choose this hospital for any of these reasons; we chose it because it was where our OB had privileges. (Something to consider when you're selecting a doctor: you should be mindful of the fact many are not employed by the hospital. This is especially true if your prenatal visits are not at the hospital itself, but at a doctor's office.) We also chose this hospital because of its proximity to our house. I have friends who have been concerned about their wife spontaneously going into labor and having to fight rush hour traffic to get to a hospital that's a half hour away. It's a valid concern for sure, but I'll take a nearby hospital with a NICU over an OB who you're enamored with every single time.

One of the nurses showed us to our room, we put some extra clothes into a drawer, I settled into the bedside recliner chair and our OB came in to restate the plan. She had a nurse start an IV drip of Pitocin – this is a drug designed to induce contractions. It would be a very slow drip, she said, as too much Pitocin can be harmful to the baby. Jenya's cervix hadn't dilated much – maybe two centimeters. The cervix needs to be dilated to 10 centimeters in order to start pushing the baby out, so we had a long way to go. We were both anxious, tired, and hungry, so we had a light meal. Then I asked the nurse to bring one of those rollaway beds into the room so I could get a little rest – turns out they were all being used (this birth center had about 25-30 rooms), so I'd be sleeping in a chair that night.

The next morning, I woke up around 6am when a nurse was performing a vaginal exam; still stuck on 2cm…not ideal. Our OB popped in before heading to her clinical office for a quick check to see how things were going. She examined Jenya as well; not much progress, she thought. While disappointing to us, the doc said it wasn't totally abnormal and inserted a small balloon into her cervix to try and help it dilate. She also suggested Jenya get up and walk around for a bit to help loosen things up. So, we went on a walk up and down the hallways of the birth unit for a little while. Me in sweats, Jenya in a hospital gown, and her IV pole on wheels, doing laps around this place. Everybody we passed in the hallways knew what we were up to, but it still felt kind of funny. We went back to the room and remained in a holding pattern, hoping things would start to progress – but there was no improvement. Around 2pm, the doctor came by and told us they were going to "manually rupture her membranes." In laymen's terms, they were going to break her water for her. I'm not quite certain what tools they used to do it, but the doctor stuck something inside of Jenya that looked like a crochet needle and within moments, a flood of liquid came pouring out of her onto the floor – I'd never seen anything like it! The good news was that it was fairly clear and odorless – a good sign that the baby wasn't in any sort of distress. They quickly mopped it all up with blue absorbent chucks pads and we felt as though we were in the next stage of labor. At that point, the lead nurse asked our doctor if they should "cut the pit;" in other words, stop the IV drip of Pitocin. Without the blink of an eye, our doctor said, "Nope." This is key – and will become important later in this book.

Not more than a couple hours after that, Jenya was starting to feel some decent pain in her pelvic area. We had discussed this prior – there was no shame in electing to have an epidural administered to relieve this pain. I've spoken with several women about their "birth plan" and the use of an epidural is always something that is discussed. I respect any woman who wants to give birth naturally, but the wuss in me says there's a good reason modern medicine includes the use of painkillers! The only caveat to the epidural is that she wouldn't be able to eat anything significant afterwards. The anesthesiologist came down to our room, walked us through the process (and had us sign consent forms), and within 20 minutes, Jenya had a giant needle in her back ready to be pumped full of a numbing agent. I could immediately sense the feeling of relief that she was experiencing, and it put me at ease, too. Guys, we will never know what it's like to give birth, but we've all experienced physical pain in our life in some way – I'm all for minimizing it as best as possible.

I went to the cafeteria to grab some food out of Jenya's sight, since she wasn't allowed to eat anything significant now that she had the epidural. I hadn't really had a moment to myself since we'd set foot in the hospital and the quiet allowed me to briefly reflect. All I could think to myself was, "Why is this taking so long? Is this normal?" I've had countless friends give birth to kids before us, and I've heard everything from, "the baby literally fell out of her when we got to the hospital" to "we were there for two days" to "we showed up and they sent us home," so I figured we were within the "normal" range. Like many guys, I'm into the stats, and according to March of Dimes, the first stage of labor for a first-time mom can last anywhere from 12-19 hours…we were approaching 24 hours. I was feeling anxious and wanting to get things moving, but our doctor and nurses kept saying Jenya's cervix was just taking its time to dilate.

After I finished my dinner, I came back to the room where Jenya and our doula were talking about next steps. This hospital's birth center provided complimentary doulas – women who specialize in being an additional support for a laboring mother…someone who has been there before. While they aren't doctors, or even nurses, they are more like birth coaches. In many parts of the world doulas are commonplace, but in the United States they are seen as a luxury item and you oftentimes will pay out of pocket for their services. Some employers have family-building benefits that cover the cost of a doula, so it's worth checking to see if you or your partner's employer has that benefit. Was I moderately offended that Jenya didn't think I could coach her by myself? Did I know that none of our friends before us had a doula in their presence during their children's births? Yes, and yes. But did I know that I signed up to do whatever reassured my wife? Most-definitely. Throughout our family-building journey, I felt as though there were some battles worth fighting, and this certainly wasn't going to be one of them.

Our doula was a nice woman, probably in her early 30s, with four kids of her own. She was a calming presence for Jenya, offering breathing tips and helping her change positions while in labor. She was also there just for us. Nurses have multiple patients to tend to, and doctors make their rounds and show up at delivery time; I understand the value of a doula, especially for first timers. She asked us if we wanted her to spend the night at the hospital with us – we told her we'd call her if things progressed, but since Jenya's dilation hadn't really moved along, we thought it best for her to go home and return in the morning.

The good news for me is that they had a cot available on the second night, which I gladly set up in our room. I was able to get a few hours of shut eye while Jenya laid and waited for things to start progressing. A nurse would come into the room every few hours to examine her cervix and check vitals. In the wee hours of the morning – maybe 2am – Jenya started to feel really lousy. The nurse confirmed that she had a fever; nearly 103 degrees. She was given some Tylenol, but combined with her not having eaten in quite some time, she was still very uncomfortable. I did my best to console her, but we were both exhausted. At this point, we'd been at the hospital for about 32 hours. We decided it would be best for us to get more rest in order to be as close to 100% when it was time for her to push in the morning. Around 6am, the nurse came in for another cervical exam…Jenya had dilated to 6cm! I was thinking, "we're actually going to have this baby soon!" The sense of relief we both felt in that moment was immense. It was probably one of the few times during our hospital stay that we felt the same way, at the same time, and that was truly special.

A couple hours later, Jenya's cervix continued to dilate, and our doctor told us it was time to push this baby out. If you've never been beside your partner when you get to this point of a labor, there are two things I can tell you: One, if she wants to hold your hand, just give her your pointer and middle finger; when she squeezes (and she will), it won't hurt as much as if she's grabbing all four of your fingers. Two, unless your partner gives you explicit permission, and you're truly interested, stand in line with her waist so you don't have to witness all that is going on south of the border. In our case, I was holding her right leg with my right arm and her right hand with my left hand. I would look at her, I would look at the doctor, I would look at the nurses…I really wanted to soak it all in without peeking into her vaginal area…but that's me (remember, I didn't do needles well before this all started). As our doctor glanced at the fetal monitoring system and witnessed an oncoming contraction, she told Jenya to "push like you're making the biggest bowel movement you've ever had." Much to my surprise, the doc was a loud cheerleader, I was encouraging her…and then the contraction passed.

A minute or so later, another contraction came on, and here we went. PUSH! YOU'VE GOT THIS! PUSH! And then the contraction passed. This went on for about 45-60 minutes. At one point, the doc said, "the baby doesn't like these contractions." Jenya asked if we were going to have a caesarean section – a surgery where they cut the woman's lower abdomen open to remove the baby from the uterus. But our doctor insisted that things were OK and there wasn't a need for that. I could tell Jenya was tired, hungry, and frustrated. This was one of those situations where as a partner, husband, and man, I wanted to be able to fix the problem, but I couldn't. It was as frustrating for me as it was for Jenya. After a few more contractions and pushes, our doctor made the recommendation to use a vacuum assist to extract the baby through the birth canal.

Let me say that again: she wanted to use what is essentially a suction cup with a rope, attach it to the baby's head inside the birth canal, and pull him out of her vagina. If it sounds crazy, that's because it just might be, despite being used for about 3% of all vaginal births in the United States. Since we had discussed it during the prenatal visits, and the doc didn't provide any alternative in that moment, we consented. The doctor unwrapped a suction cup attached to a rope, with a handle on the other end that the doc would squeeze. The doctor had a mild look of confusion, but a nurse helped her assemble a few parts. Then, she took the suction cup and stuck it inside of Jenya, presumably on our baby's head. After that, she squeezed the handle a few times to create a seal on the suction cup. Finally, when the next contraction came, she got into what I would call a somewhat athletic stance, made the rope taut, and pulled with what seemed to be an incredible amount of force. If you've ever watched one of those Strongman competitions, it was like she was trying to pull a tractor with this thing. But the suction cup popped off the baby's head. So, it was back to square one: re-attach the suction cup, squeeze the handle, get ready for the next contraction…and start pulling. And it popped off again! She tried to attach the vacuum a third time, but before she even tried to pull, it happened.

"WE'VE GOT TO GO, NOW," exclaimed the doctor.

And within seconds, Jenya was unhooked from the monitors, and was being wheeled into the operating room.

Labor was medically induced using Pitocin (a synthetic form of oxytocin), which was administered via a slow IV drip due to the potential risks of overstimulation. Pitocin is commonly used during inductions but MUST be monitored closely to ensure both mom and baby are safe.

Jenya received an epidural to manage increasing pain during labor. Following epidural administration by the anesthesiologist, she was no longer able to eat full meals. Regular cervical checks and vital sign monitoring were performed; a maternal fever (103°F) was detected and treated with Tylenol and antibiotics.

After over 30 hours of labor, Jenya began pushing. When fetal distress was noted ("the baby doesn't like these contractions"), a vacuum-assisted delivery was attempted multiple times but failed, as the suction cup detached repeatedly.

According to a study published in American Journal of Obstetrics & Gynecology, vacuum extraction was successful in 95% of deliveries of babies in the "sunny side up" position. That said, 10% of babies have facial or scalp lacerations and up to 38% have a retinal hemorrhage, which may or may not affect vision. I'm not a doctor, but knowing what I know, I would never recommend a vacuum-assisted delivery.

Emergency Cesarean Section: Due to failed vacuum extraction attempts and signs of fetal distress, the OB made the rapid decision to move Jenya to the operating room for an emergency C-section.

Chapter Six

I was now alone with our doula in the labor and delivery room, when she said, "let me go get you some scrubs." She brought me a shirt and pants that were three sizes too big and told me to follow her to the operating room. We went down the hall, and she told me to hang tight while she went to see if I could head into the operating room. While I waited for her to come back, a rush of other medical staff was going into the O.R.; some were wheeling equipment, others just moving themselves at an unusually brisk pace. I didn't recognize any of them. It was like a scene out of a movie. It wasn't chaos, but there was a definite sense of urgency, as if something wasn't right. Not more than a minute went by when the doula came back and said, "they can't have you in there right now." I was staring at a set of double doors, my wife and unborn child on the other side, and I couldn't go inside. I was helpless, scared, anxious, and upset. I paced back and forth in a small space near a water cooler. My in-laws and my mother were at our house, awaiting good news, and I had to call and tell them what was happening.

"Mom, there's a problem," I said after she answered her phone.

"Is the baby here?" she asked.

"Just get here. Bring everyone. I don't know anything else right now." I know she wanted to know more, but I didn't have anything else to tell her. The doula and a nurse came out and asked me if I needed anything – what was I supposed to say? Of course I needed something, you morons…I needed my wife and my son! I was shivering, crying, and in mental agony. After what seemed like an eternity, but was actually just 10 minutes later, a nurse emerged from behind the double doors.

"Matt, your wife is OK."

I'd never felt so relieved in my life than to hear those words.

"But what about the baby?" I asked.

"They're still working on the baby," she replied. "I'll be back with an update when I have one."

That seemed very odd to me. My wife is OK, but there's no news on the human you just cut out of her? I was still nervous and scared. After another 10 minutes went by, a man I had never met emerged from behind the double doors.

"Matt, my name is Dr. Y., and I'm the on-call neonatologist. Your son had a very rough delivery. You're going to get to see him in a little bit, but you need to know that we are going to transport him to the NICU (neonatal intensive care unit) at our hospital downtown."

"What happened?" I asked, like any other father would who has yet to meet his just-born son.

"Your son was born without a heartbeat," he explained. "The team worked on him for 14 minutes to resuscitate him, and he's now hooked up to oxygen and is going to be placed into a cooling protocol to try and minimize any brain damage."

I was in shock. He told me I'd be able to see my wife in the recovery room, and I was finally escorted through the double doors, past some other people who looked like EMTs, and into a room where a just-out-of-general anesthesia-Jenya was laying on a gurney. She was half asleep when I came in and hugged her.

"Where's the baby?" she asked me.

A nurse overheard her and told us both that we'd get to see him in a few minutes, as they were getting him situated in the isolette (clear, plastic enclosed crib) for an ambulance ride downtown. Jenya and I embraced for a bit, really unsure of the gravity of the situation. Then, moments later, a couple of uniformed EMTs rolled a plexiglass box up to us…and inside of it lay our newborn son, connected to tubes and oxygen. Welcome to the world, Benjamin Gino. Instead of holding him in our arms, and placing him on mom's chest, we were sticking our hands through these little holes to give him a quick caress before the EMTs loaded him into an ambulance. These were not the newborn pictures we had expected to take.

Jenya had just had major emergency surgery, so unfortunately our decision was made for us: I would go downtown to be with our son while she recovered at the birth hospital. To say she wasn't happy about that would be the understatement of the decade. My in-laws stayed with Jenya while my mom and I stopped at the house so I could quickly shower and grab some clothes and toiletries, knowing I'd be at the hospital downtown for several days. My mom and I have a solid relationship – as much as she wanted to ask me a ton of questions, she knew I was in no mood to talk while we drove the 20 minutes downtown. Upon arrival, we were directed to an elevator that would get us to the NICU. The lighting was somewhat dim – there were about a dozen patient rooms arranged in a semi-circle around the nurses' station. Dr. Y. and some nurses greeted us and showed us where Benjamin was staying.

The cooling protocol was underway – when I saw Benjamin for the first time out of his isolette, his limbs and chest were wrapped in something that could be described as tiny bubble wrap, with the cords and cables affixed to him popping out from the bottom of the vest. In reality, it was a cool pack, designed to lower his body temperature a few degrees to attempt to stave off any brain damage from the rough delivery. He was also hooked up to a breathing tube and a few other monitors. Benjamin didn't make any noise, didn't move much, and was certainly not in a position to be held. I caressed his limbs and just looked at him – this was not the "dad" experience I had envisioned. His sweet face was expressionless, there was no crying to try to soothe, and there was nothing I could do to help him – it was the exact opposite of what I thought this day would entail. His nurse had to prick his heel to draw blood – this is fairly common in newborns – but because his core temperature was colder than normal, it was trickier for her to actually get the blood out of him. My mom was with me, and I relayed as many details as I could to Jenya via text message. My rabbi offered to bring me dinner. He came by and we chatted for a while. He told me he'd had some experience with this before and that it was very early for us to know anything. Later that night, a pediatric neurologist from Children's Hospital came by to examine Benjamin. She told me they'd be running some more tests on him, and we'd know more in the morning.

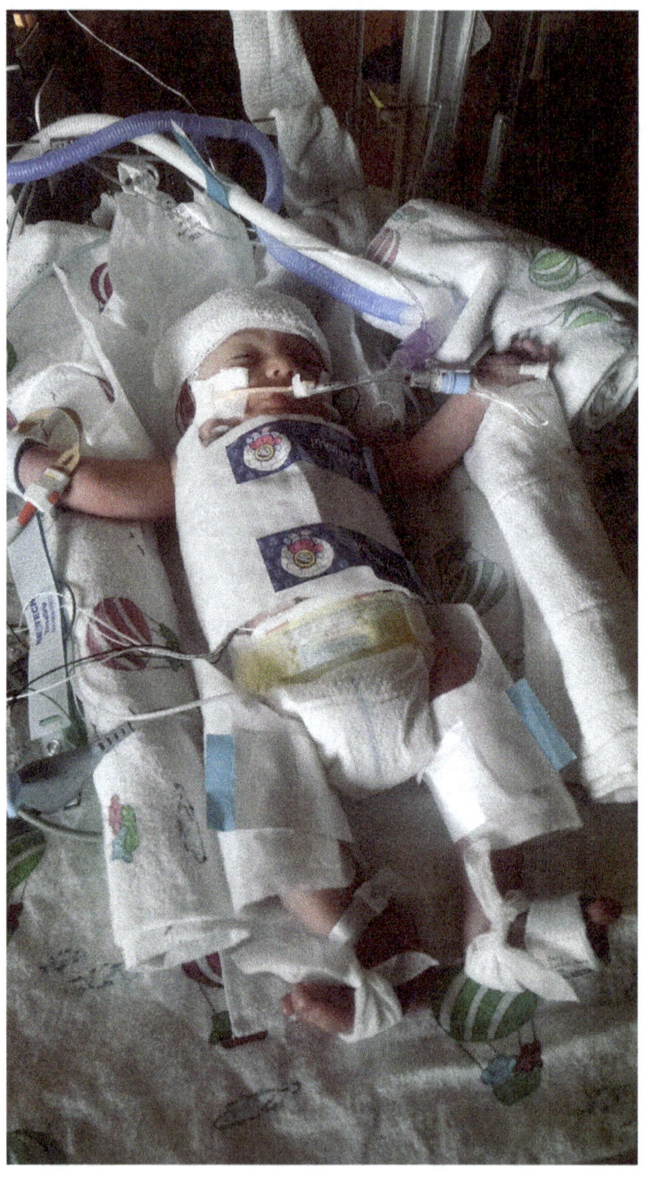

Meanwhile, at the hospital 15 miles away, Jenya was recovering in the room in which she was supposed to have delivered our son. Fortunately, she was surrounded by her parents and another one of our rabbis, but she was missing the one person she thought she'd be holding in her arms. We spoke on the phone a couple of times that evening, trying to process everything that we had been through over the past 12 hours. She was hopped up on painkillers, and I was mentally and physically exhausted. I shared as much as I could with her, but I knew she wished our family could be together – we both did. I laid down on the sofa bed next to my son to try and get some rest, unsure of what was to come.

The next morning, I met another one of the neonatologists who explained that Benjamin's blood gas level had normalized. But the pediatric neurologist would be coming over to walk me through the next steps. She explained that hooking him up to an EEG – this is where they connect about 25-30 electrodes to the scalp to measure electrical activity in the brain – would be the best way to determine our next course of action. But we'd be going to Children's Hospital to do this, as they have staff that can monitor brain activity 24/7. Remember the four NICU levels I discussed earlier – Children's Hospital is the only Level IV NICU in the state, and that's where Benjamin needed to be. I was going to take the first ambulance ride of my life, with my son in the back. I grabbed my duffel bag and sat in the front passenger seat of the rig while three EMTs were tending to Benjamin in the back. No lights, no sirens, just a 20-minute drive across town to Children's. We pulled up into an area that was reserved for ambulances and were escorted through some doors, down a hallway to an elevator. Benjamin was wheeled away, and I was shown to a waiting area where I'd eventually be met by the attending physician, Dr. LG.

"Congratulations on the birth of your son," she said. I was somewhat stunned that those were the first words to come out of her mouth. I'd soon hear similar sentiments from other health care workers at this hospital, so it is clearly part of their training. She went on to explain that Benjamin suffered quite an injury during delivery, and the EEG would help us learn if he was having seizures as well as determine how much brain activity he had. She ushered me into the NICU, via a locked entry door. I would later receive my "parent" badge that I would have to flash at a security camera while ringing a doorbell to be let into this area. It was bright, spacious, and felt exactly like a place where I'd want my son or daughter to heal. As I entered the room, nurses were gluing electrodes to Benjamin's head. He was still in his cooling blanket and still hadn't made a sound. I was just soaking it all in, learning more about neonatal medicine than I ever expected to. In addition to the attending physician and nurses, there were respiratory therapists, occupational therapists, dieticians, lactation consultants, specialists…and residents. Children's Hospital of Wisconsin is affiliated with the Medical College of Wisconsin, which means resident physicians are part of the care team and rotate through the NICU as part of their training. Some of the residents I met with were quite knowledgeable and competent; others I wish I could've smacked across the head once or twice. But in many hospital settings, it's part of the deal and you come to accept it.

The official diagnosis was hypoxic ischemic encephalopathy, known as HIE. To the layperson, it's a type of brain damage that occurs due to a lack of oxygen or blood flow to the brain before, during, or shortly after birth. Of course, with smart phone in hand, it was quite easy to find out that the prognosis for a newborn with HIE ranges from long-term disabilities to death. One NIH article says 40-60% of affected infants die by two years of age[1]. With the help of family and friends, I quickly started making connections with parents of other children who had similar births and gleaned quite a bit of information. One woman in particular, whose son was 8 years old, said something that will stick with me forever: "He can't walk, he can't talk, and he needs help with everything, but he has a smile that lights up the room." She told me not to believe the doctors that doubted my son. In the moment, it was comforting to have that kind of encouragement. A former colleague of mine, whose son was born at 24 weeks and has Cerebral Palsy, explained to me that they were in the NICU with him for three months. He told me, "You're going to have bad days, terrible days, and then some good days. Make sure to get plenty of sleep and let the nurses and doctors do the work for you."

Jenya was on her way over, having received special permission to leave her recovery room for a few hours to spend time with her

---

1. https://pmc.ncbi.nlm.nih.gov/articles/PMC3171747/

newborn. Mind you, she had a major abdominal surgery less than 48 hours prior…normally after a C-section, a woman is bed-ridden for at least 3-4 days. Her mom wheeled her into the NICU room; I was thrilled to see her and she told me how happy she was to be there. She also told me – I'll never forget this – that she loved how much I stepped up and handled everything by myself, without her being there. It made this new dad VERY happy to know that he did right by his wife, considering the circumstances. Jenya asked the doc if she could hold Benjamin. We moved her into a recliner and then with the help of two nurses and a respiratory therapist, lifted Benjamin, his EEG cords, his breathing tube, and everything else he was connected to from his basinet and into his mom's arms. Our seven-pound baby weighed 3-4 times as much…I know, because I took a turn with him too.

I created a group message thread to provide updates to family and friends. While Jenya was holding Ben Gino, I was letting everyone know that his kidneys were functioning, his limbs and eyes were more reactive, and we'd know more after his induced hypothermia – the cooling protocol – came to an end. It was Super Bowl Sunday, and I was getting ready to watch the big game.

Super Bowl 51 was one for the ages. Tom Brady and the New England Patriots scored 19 fourth-quarter points to force overtime and scored in overtime to beat the Atlanta Falcons 34-28. For much of America, it was one of the greatest comebacks in NFL history. But in NICU room 7015, where I was watching the game with my two-day old son, I made it pretty clear to him: "Benjamin, you're going to be the greatest comeback in history."

An unplanned C-section is just that – unplanned. As a dad or dad-to-be, it's going to be on you to stay emotionally level because your partner is going to be in physical pain, mental fog, or likely a combination of the two. Having a doula or support person can help navigate the chaos, but emotional resilience is essential when plans change suddenly.

Benjamin was officially diagnosed with HIE, a serious condition resulting from oxygen deprivation to the brain around the time of birth. We didn't know that until all of the chaos had subsided. If you can find a way to relay key medical information clearly to other family members, especially when communication is limited, it will help. In moments of crisis, sharing only confirmed facts and maintaining calm can prevent additional stress – easier said than done.

Advocate and stay engaged in your newborn's care, even if it feels overwhelming. Learning medical terms, asking questions, and building rapport with doctors and nurses can help you feel more in control and better support your child. Plus, it will allow you to be the strong, active parent you want to be.

Accept help and celebrate small moments of connection, like touching your baby or being able to hold them for the first time. These moments matter deeply and recognizing them helps build emotional strength during prolonged hospital stays. Take each day as a blessing and cherish every moment.

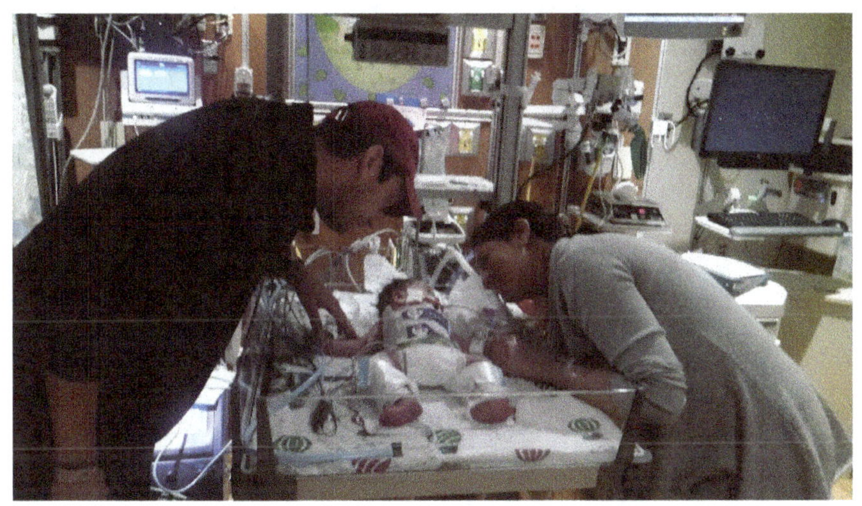

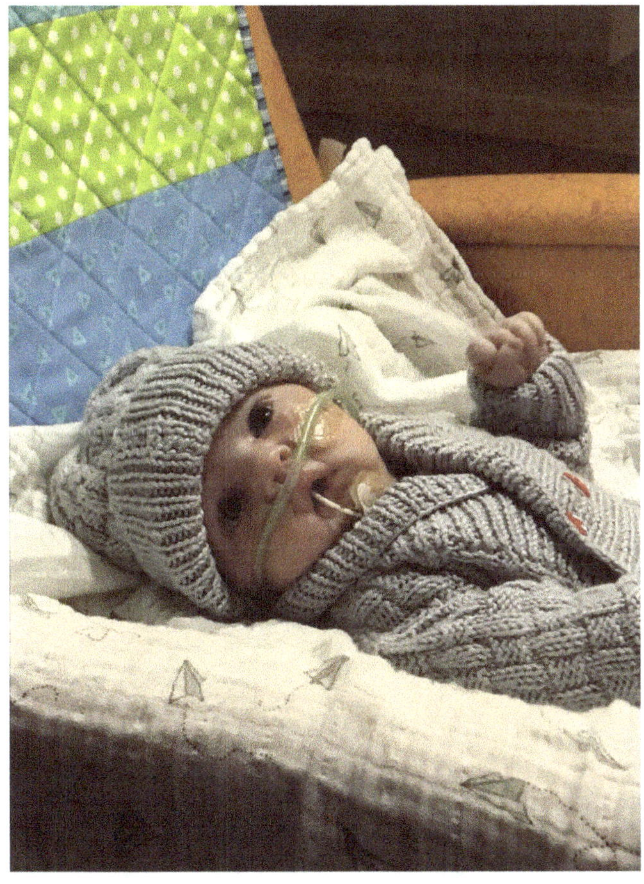

Chapter Seven

After three days of wearing the cooling blanket, it was time to get Benjamin's body temperature back to 98.6 degrees and see how his brain would respond. The doctors tried to pull the breathing tube and unfortunately, he didn't respond well. In fact, a "code blue" was called and several doctors and nurses swarmed into the room. I was there when it happened, speaking with the hospital chaplain, and I burst into tears. They were able to reintubate Benjamin and stabilize his breathing, but it was certainly traumatic for me. On day four, Jenya was discharged from her hospital and was able to join me full-time in the NICU. It was wonderful to have her by my side as we began our life together as parents, albeit under very trying circumstances.

Benjamin started to make some arm and leg movements, but we came to learn that these were tied to seizures. Each ensuing day would bring more examinations, more tests, more specialists, and more waiting. Children's had a family sleeping room for parents who either lived out of town or had an extended stay; we were fortunate enough to be given a chance to use it several of the nights we were in the NICU. Having previously watched "The Bachelor" together while we were dating, Jenya and I decided to call this unassuming, hospital grade bedroom the "fantasy suite."

On day 10, an MRI was scheduled. We escorted Benjamin, along with members of his care team, down to the radiology department at the hospital where he was wheeled into an MRI suite. There was no guarantee they would get a good result because it's difficult for an infant to stay still—but we had to try. After about 20 minutes of waiting, I was informed that they got a clean test and we'd be speaking with the neurologist later that day.

Around mid-day, one of the neurology residents came to look at Benjamin as part of his routine. The resident mentioned that he heard the MRI went well, and the damage to the basal ganglia, towards the middle of the brain, was repairable. We were relieved! Jenya and I had a glimmer of hope that our boy would eventually be able to come home; we knew it wouldn't be easy, but he was going to have a life. The resident told us our staff neurologist would be by later in the afternoon to talk about next steps and to give us the full readout of the MRI.

When the neurologist entered the room a few hours later, he

was stone-faced. We were confused; the resident had just told us things could be repaired.

"Residents," muttered Dr. W., our neurologist. "He spoke out of turn. The thalamus, attached to the basal ganglia, was severely damaged. Without it, nothing else can self-repair."

We went from relief to devastation in a matter of two hours. Our attending physician was in the room shortly after we heard this.

"So, what does this mean for Benjamin?" I asked.

"He probably won't walk, he will need a feeding tube, he won't talk, and he will need supplemental oxygen to survive long term."

I looked to Jenya, looked at the doctor, and asked a question that less than a week ago was unimaginable to even think: "Should we be thinking about…terminating his life?"

"We're not terminating his life," explained the attending physician, "but we can modify his care plan to let nature take its course. This is not an easy decision to make, and we have a palliative care team here to help you. Why don't we have a care conference to discuss all of this."

Of course they had a name for it: Care Conference. They had a name for everything; why would this be any different? We gathered in a room just outside the NICU that was literally designed for these types of meetings. It was a small conference room, with enough chairs for all the docs that needed to attend and some soft seating for the parents and family members who were about to hear some of the worst news of their lives. Jenya and I asked a few questions about how this would look. We were told Benjamin would probably live for a few more weeks—maybe longer, maybe shorter—depending on how much support was withheld. It was recommended to us that we see how he does without supplemental oxygen. He had gone from a breathing tube to a nasal canula a few days prior, so we elected to let him simply breathe the air in the room, like you and I do.

Shortly after we made the decision, we brought our parents into the conference room to share the results of the MRI and the prognosis. It was the first time I cried in front of my parents in a long, long time…and unfortunately, it wouldn't be the last in the days to come. A couple days later, the weather turned unseasonably warm for February, and the hospital had a photographer visit us to take family pictures. There is a non-profit called *Now I Lay Me Down To Sleep* that has an army of volunteer photographers who take pictures of deceased and terminally ill babies. We were able to bring Benjamin outside into the hospital's healing garden for a family photo shoot. After we came back in, we took a few more; the photographer had each of us hold him clothed and unclothed, because who doesn't like to see a cute baby in the flesh. When Jenya was holding him, Benjamin made it clear he was done with the photo session by pooping all over the floor and her jeans! He might not have been able to speak, but he sure could communicate!

The next day, we met with the director of the palliative care team to learn a little more about how things would progress. We were informed that we could have morphine administered to Benjamin to eliminate the possibility of any pain he might be feeling. Without hesitation, we gave the docs the green light. What we were told could take up to two weeks took less than 24 hours: after 17 days on Earth, Benjamin succumbed to his injuries and passed away in our arms on February 20, 2017.

* * *

I will always remember walking into our congregation's sanctuary for the funeral. Holding Jenya's hand, my head was down as I didn't want people to see my red, watery eyes. Out of my periphery, I could see that there were a lot of people in attendance – in the hundreds, I was told. We were escorted to the front row, about 10 feet away from a white, closed casket that was no more than three feet long. Our rabbi and my brother-in-law both shared some words, including the parents' prayer that Jenya and I had written before he was born and the words we put together after he passed away. I was sobbing uncontrollably for what felt like an eternity – imagine seeing a 36-year-old man crying loudly in an otherwise quiet space, it doesn't happen very often. It happened on that day, and it changed me forever.

Before Benjamin's delivery, in anticipation of this life-changing moment in our lives, our rabbi had advised us to write a parents' prayer for him to be read at his baby naming. We did…and then had to write a eulogy a couple weeks later. Here they are in their entirety:

Dear Ben Gino,

We wrote this prayer for you before you arrived. We planned to read it at your bris. "Welcome to the world little one. We love you so much already. We have prayed so much for you to be here with us, safe and healthy. For your life we pray for you to be thoughtful and kind. To be ambitious, convicted and driven in whatever you choose. To take steps forward each day and to be OK to change direction when that makes sense. We pray for you to develop a strong rudder to guide you as you explore this world because you will almost certainly be curious. We pray for you to dream big and to have the focus to achieve your goals, and not to mistake dreams for goals. We pray for you to find love in family, friends, and someday in a partner. We pray for you to be comfortable being uncomfortable. To try things, to risk, to make mistakes and to always persevere. Life will not be easy but it will be worth it. The lowest times will make the highest times that much more meaningful and joyous. We pray for you to wonder, aspire, and to be grateful the way we are so grateful for you."

Benjamin Gino, your life didn't turn out the way we planned but that in itself is a lesson in parenting. At first we were scared and angry that you were brought into the world like this to suffer and be poked and prodded your whole life. But we are so grateful we got to know your big eyes and beautiful face and body. To know your sassy spirit. In your 17 days you have taught us so much. You taught us about love. You taught us what it means to love someone unconditionally and deeply. When we held you for the first time you were covered in EEG leads and tubes and cords. Still, it was the best feeling in the world to hold you. It was what we had dreamed of doing forever. You taught us to love you deeply and our hearts grew immeasurably for you and for each other.

You taught us to trust and rely on others. We learned to lean on others, to ask for help and to allow others to love us. We learned how strong and loving our community is here. Our Milwaukee family is stronger than we could have imagined. You taught us about love.

You taught us about levity. When we got to take pictures of you we asked to take a picture of your cute tush. As I stood proudly holding you up, I felt warmth all down my leg. "Is he peeing?" I asked your dad. Dad said "nope!" that's not pee. You had pooped all down my leg. Thank you for fully indoctrinating us into parenthood. After you passed away, dad was holding you. I was on the phone with the organ donation organization. They had an hour's worth of questions to ask us so we could donate your heart valves. After 30 minutes of exhausting questions they told me they had more questions but they might not be age appropriate. Ok, I said. "Does he have any tattoos?" they asked me. "He better not" I thought. "Has he done heroin?" they asked me. "Not to my knowledge," I said. Seeing as we are in temple, we will spare you the detailed questions they asked about your sexual history. Thanks for the laughs, buddy. In the darkest moments of our life, we were able to laugh for a moment. To imagine you with tattoos and a rather sordid life at 17 days.

You taught us most about bravery. You were so brave. You endured more than most people endure in a lifetime. You taught us to be brave. When the doctors told us what your life could be like we didn't think we could survive. We couldn't ease your pain. That was the worst feeling, to see you suffering and not be able to scoop you up and snuggle you and protect you. You taught us to be brave. To make it through the next minute, hour, and day. To keep reading to you, and singing to you, and giving you baths, and talking to your doctors and digesting so much information. Too much information. You taught us to move forward each day. And we will continue to be brave for you. To make your memory a blessing. To honor you in all the ways we can think of. You did big things on this earth during your 17 days and we will always do big things in your name. We are so inspired by you. You have deeply touched the hearts of our friends and family and of all of the doctors and nurses who worked with you. We love you. We are grateful for you.

Rest in peace and comfort, Ben Gino. We love you. We will be thinking of you always. Thank you for making us parents.

Love, Mom and Dad.

* * *

In the days following the funeral, we were surrounded by family and friends. But more importantly, Jenya and I immediately sought counseling. In the words of our rabbi, we couldn't let our emotions "hit a brick wall" and needed to get out in front of our grief. We went to therapy sessions weekly for quite some time; eventually, we reduced the frequency of these visits. To say they saved our marriage is an understatement. There were definitely moments over those initial weeks following Benjamin's death where I wondered what the future held: for me, for us, for our potential family. We were processing feelings at different stages, through different lenses. It was impossible for us to truly understand what the other was feeling and by having an expert in the room with us, she acted as "translator" so we could better understand each other and move forward together. My love for Jenya was as strong as it had ever been at the end of each of our sessions. Dr. K., our psychologist, is someone for whom we will be forever grateful.

About three months after the loss, we decided to start trying again. Jenya didn't feel ready but was concerned since she was now 40 years old, that if we didn't start trying, it wouldn't happen for us. I was absolutely ready to pick ourselves up and continue to try building the family we so desperately wanted. This was a regular topic of conversation in our therapy sessions; we both knew we weren't getting any younger, but it was evident that the grief process was a heavier load for Jenya than it was for me. Dr. K. helped us create the space to grieve Benjamin while also working towards our ultimate goal of having a healthy, living child.

It was back to the fertility clinic for another round of IVF, which meant another round of Jenya injecting herself (or me injecting her) with synthetic hormones. Of course, that meant more mood swings – while we were dealing with our grief. We were mourning our son while trying so terribly hard to start a family; and I wasn't the one trying to grow a baby inside of me. I will never be able to fully understand what she was going through, but at the time, I got the sense that Jenya felt so much pressure to deliver, both literally and figuratively, that it became a near impossibility. The IVF transfer went fine, but the implantation resulted in nothing more than a chemical pregnancy. We were back to square one, once again. The gut-punch we both felt had us wondering if we were doing the right thing. Maybe we should've explored adoption. Maybe kids weren't in the cards for us. Maybe we just needed a new plan.

Get clarity from multiple medical professionals before forming expectations. Residents and attending physicians may interpret test results differently. Always ask to speak with senior staff for a comprehensive and accurate understanding of diagnoses and prognoses.

Utilize palliative care teams early when facing difficult decisions. They are specifically trained to support families through end-of-life care, helping you understand options, prioritizing comfort, and making choices that align with your values. Many hospitals can also provide chaplains who align with your religious views.

Take opportunities to create meaningful memories, even during terminal care. Engaging with organizations like March of Dimes or participating in photo sessions will create special moments and offer lasting comfort to preserve your child's legacy. Many families have photos of their deceased children throughout their homes — it's important that everyone knows these babies are an eternal part of their families and never forgotten.

Allow space for open emotional expression and community support. Sharing grief with loved ones, whether through a funeral, storytelling, or communal rituals, helps process unimaginable loss and reminds you that you are not alone.

Chapter Eight

Our primary fertility doctor was a brutally honest man. I appreciated it, but many others thought his bedside manner could've been softened a bit. Perhaps it was because he was less than a year from retiring, and perhaps it was because his job was to deal with stressed, sensitive, and highly emotional women on a daily basis. But he said to Jenya point blank: "if your goal is to have a healthy child, you need to use an egg donor." It was something that had been brought up to us after previous failed cycles, but Jenya didn't want to accept that as our only option. And how could she? Now, she was ready to move forward with a donor. It was a huge step forward for her, and I'm so thankful that she came to the realization that living children, whether genetically related or not, would still be hers.

The clinic had several donors on their roster who were willing to commit to a round of IVF for a fee. Our clinic only did what are called "closed donations," in that we would never meet each other nor learn of each other's identity. There are other places where you can have an "open donation," and meet the donor. Of course, you could also find an egg donor on your own and explore that route, but that wasn't something we were looking to pursue. I remember having that conversation with Jenya – there was talk of a friend of hers who might have been willing to donate eggs, but I really didn't think that was in anyone's best interests…and I didn't want to be the father to a child of whom I knew the biological mother. To find a donor, we sifted through an electronic catalogue of sorts. There were pictures of the donors, biological information about their family background, health history, careers, you name it. We knew their sexual orientation, their parents' and grandparents' health, and their religion. Basically, everything you'd want to know about your partner before you had kids with them…except their name and address. Jenya and I agreed we wanted a donor with dark hair and features similar to hers – the two of us weren't producing a blonde baby anytime soon! We narrowed the list down to two donors and then decided to do a "pros and cons" list for each. After much deliberation, we ended up selecting donor #123 *(fictitious number for privacy)*.

And just like that, with our deposit made, our fertility clinic lined up our donor to do an egg retrieval cycle. We knew the drill, but the buildup to retrieval day was certainly anxiety-producing. We had already spent thousands of dollars on our own infertility journey – now we were paying for someone else to give us a batch of eggs. Would they be good enough? Would they fertilize? Would Jenya's body be able to carry them?

We got the call shortly after retrieval day – 21 eggs! We were ecstatic. THIS is how IVF is supposed to go for a healthy, 20-something woman. The clinic told us to be ready for a transfer in four days, as they were fertilizing the eggs with my sperm, and we could expect more than a couple to grow into viable embryos. On day five, we arrived at the clinic to learn that we had 11 viable embryos. Embryos are graded or evaluated on a few key features, including how much they have grown and developed, the quality of the cells that will become the baby, and the quality of the outer layer of cells that will form the placenta. Doctors use these ratings to determine which one(s) to transfer to a woman's uterus for the best possible outcome. That said, some doctors will tell you that the letter grade is not the "be all, end all" to determine which embryo(s) to transfer. Some women will have multiple embryos transferred to increase the odds of a successful pregnancy, although this is increasingly less common as it can put the mother and babies at greater risk. This is why there are more twins and triplets in today's world than ever before. Because Jenya is a higher-risk carrier, we stuck with a single embryo transfer.

You know the routine now; so did we. Each transfer is filled with some anticipation, some excitement, and plenty of anxiety. Will it work? What is this embryo going to be like? Will Jenya handle the pregnancy any better or worse than the ones before?

Would the fact that this child wouldn't be genetically related to her effect how she went about things? I know it bothered Jenya a bit, but I have to give my wife a ton of credit; she continued to have the mindset that nurture is just as important (if not more) than nature. Not to mention, this baby was going to be growing inside of her, with her blood.

The transfer went well, and the wait was on to see if the embryo would "stick" and grow. Speaking of sticks, you better believe we went through more than a few boxes of pregnancy tests in the days ahead, before the ultrasound to confirm a heartbeat. Each day I was greeted with a smile, a positive mood, and a great deal of hope. Jenya had a good feeling about this one, and the sticks were confirming her suspicion. So did the ultrasound – at six weeks, we went to the fertility clinic to see a screen with a flashing star – that heartbeat was as strong as ever, and we were pregnant again! The doctor and nurses were thrilled for us and once again, we were discharged to our primary OB.

Egg donation can significantly improve IVF outcomes in certain cases: For women with repeated failed cycles or poor egg quality, using a donor egg—especially from a young, healthy donor—can dramatically increase the chances of successful fertilization and pregnancy.

Embryo grading helps guide transfer decisions but isn't absolute: Embryos are graded (typically A, B, or C) based on quality, but lower-grade embryos can still result in healthy pregnancies. Doctors use this system to optimize selection but often emphasize that it's not a perfect predictor.

Single embryo transfer is often recommended for high-risk pregnancies: Transferring just one embryo reduces the risks associated with multiple gestations, which can be especially important for women with medical conditions or higher-risk pregnancy histories.

Psychological readiness is crucial in donor-assisted reproduction: It's important to consider the emotional and psychological aspects of using a donor, including acceptance of the lack of genetic connection and ensuring both partners are on the same page before proceeding. It's quite possible you and/or your partner will undergo a psychiatric evaluation before a fertility clinic allows you to proceed.

Chapter Nine

As one might imagine, Jenya and I agreed that we'd be going to a different obstetrician moving forward. We both felt a great amount of anger towards the previous doctor. I could write an entire book about those feelings and some of the thoughts that went through my head, but they are neither healthy nor worth sharing. Let's just say, I'm glad she and her family moved halfway across the world a few years after Benjamin's death. Our therapist, who we continued to see throughout this current pregnancy, had referred us to some doctors at the large academic hospital in which she worked. Jenya and I spoke with each of them and also received some feedback from others about them. We determined that a man who we'll refer to as Dr. L. would be our OB moving forward.

Our first visit with Dr. L. took on a much different tone than our first visit with our previous provider. He was exceptionally empathetic to our situation and overall fertility journey. He told us he'd worked with patients with similar high-risk histories, and that he was going to do everything in his power to keep both of us at ease. He promised to order every test and perform every ultrasound necessary to keep my anxious wife as sane as possible over the next 7.5 months. I felt especially reassured in that he was forthright in telling us that he would always be concerned about this pregnancy…there was no laissez faire attitude about things, which was how I felt at times with our previous doctor. Additionally, he recognized that there were two partners in the room, which I greatly appreciated. In other words, he said and did all the right things, and Jenya and I both left that meeting feeling good about our decision to select him as our new OB.

Around 12 weeks into the pregnancy, we went in for a Nuchal translucency (NT) ultrasound, as well as a battery of genetic tests. The NT scan helps determine a baby's risk of congenital conditions, such as Down syndrome, by measuring the amount of fluid behind the baby's neck. Our new hospital also had a thorough genetic testing program, of which we took full advantage. There are a handful of tests out there, and with our history, we wanted the most-comprehensive battery of tests to help determine the viability of this baby. Good news all around; the NT scan showed no issues, and our genetic bloodwork came back normal – all was progressing as it should.

Throughout this pregnancy, we continued to see our therapist who would be able to communicate with Dr. L. about any emotions Jenya and I were feeling and the issues we were having. Partners reading this book, I can tell you first-hand that having a third-party act as a "translator" of sorts is incredibly beneficial. The hormones inside a pregnant woman are nothing to be messed with; in fact, I started calling them "her-mones" just to provide a little levity! Of course, I was anxious as well, but I always maintained a mindset that we had already experienced the worst possible situation – the odds of this happening again were so miniscule, I didn't even think about it. I've almost always put logic ahead of emotion, and in this case, it just made sense to do that. Jenya and I shared far more moments of positivity after our therapy sessions and were almost always on the same page when we'd leave the office.

At 20 weeks, we went in for the anatomy scan. This is the high-tech ultrasound that can provide 3D images of your baby which make him or her look like an alien. Everything looked normal on this scan: ten fingers, ten toes, plus limbs and a head that measured appropriately. In addition, we confirmed the gender (a boy), and were feeling very good about the growth of the baby. The plan moving forward was just like Benjamin's plan. We would get routine ultrasounds, and if there was any spotting (minimal bleeding) coming from Jenya, we'd monitor her closely and head to the hospital if it didn't let up.

Jenya was hooked on salmon during this pregnancy; certainly, a healthier option than the Dairy Queen she was craving before!

As the baby grew inside of her, she was feeling him kick and move around…anything to reassure her that things were tracking in the right direction was a win for both of us. We would go in for ultrasounds more often than a normal pregnancy just to have some peace of mind. Dr. L. was always supportive of our wishes and as we approached the third trimester, we looked at the calendar to schedule a C-section. In a high-risk pregnancy with a mother who is over 35, there is evidence that the chance of a stillbirth doubles between week 39 and week 40 (40 being a full-term pregnancy).[1] Jenya had also developed placenta previa, which is a condition when the placenta blocks all or a portion of the cervix. We pushed our doctor to schedule the C-section at 37 weeks…his only issue was reworking a planned trip out of town as this would be leading into Memorial Day weekend. He told us he was 99% certain he'd be around in the morning to take care of us, but he didn't want to guarantee it. That was good enough for us – this baby was coming out of Jenya's belly on May 24!

The furniture was ordered…again. The nursery was painted… again. We were all-systems go. Ultrasounds were taking place each week, along with NSTs, and everything looked just fine. On May 17, I got ready for work just like I do every day: shave, shower, get dressed, and head downstairs for a bowl of cereal and a glass of orange juice. But as I was about to spoon the first

---

1. Risk of stillbirth in older mothers: a specific delivery plan might be considered for prevention, 2022

bite of Cheerios into my mouth, Jenya called out to me, "Matt, I'm bleeding!"

"You're bleeding?" I couldn't believe it.

"We have to go to the hospital…now," she said.

Without traffic, the hospital where we were to deliver is about 25 minutes from our house…but it was 7:30am, morning rush hour…and I was concerned. She came downstairs, drank my orange juice to get the baby kicking, and we got in the car, cell phone chargers in hand (but no overnight bags). I white-knuckled it to the hospital in just over 30 minutes…I've never bobbed and weaved through traffic quite like that. Jenya called the OB department while we were in the car to let them know we were en route. I pulled up to the Emergency Department entrance as we were instructed, and helped her inside, where a wheelchair was waiting. We were both visibly upset…and for the first time in eight months, I was scared we were going to have a stillbirth. A nurse reassured us that we got there in plenty of time, and everything was going to be OK.

We were guided through a maze of hallways and up to the labor and delivery department, and then into a triage room. Jenya was connected to some monitors and we immediately heard the baby's heartbeat. That was the sound of relief we both needed to calm down and it was at that point that we were officially "in line" for a delivery.

Remember, this is a large academic hospital and since we weren't having the C-section on our scheduled date, there was no telling who was going to deliver our baby; there are more than 20 OBs who work at this hospital. Another nurse popped into our room and said, "Dr. L. will be in to check on you shortly." We looked at each other and were like, "He's working today? It's gotta be a sign that this is meant to be!"

A few minutes later, in waltzed Dr. L. and, with his usual wit, he said, "You guys *really* wanted to make sure I was gonna be the one to deliver this baby, huh?" He reassured us that we did the right thing by coming today, and that even though the two operating rooms were tied up, we'd have a baby in our arms within two hours. Shortly after he departed the room, I texted all of our parents and our rabbi that things were in motion. Nurses continued to monitor Jenya, who wasn't having any contractions or feeling any discomfort, because she wasn't in actual labor. There's no doubt in either of our minds that the emotional discomfort far outweighed any physical discomfort she was feeling throughout the morning.

About an hour later, a nurse told us they were prepping the operating room for our C-section and that she and a few others would be back to wheel in Jenya shortly. I was given scrubs, booties, and a hat to wear as I'd be escorted in once they had begun the procedure. Just putting on this protective gear without a rush, knowing that I'd be able to be in the room with my wife, I was already crying tears of joy, and we didn't even have a baby in our arms! As I was getting dressed, in walked our rabbi – we couldn't believe he came to the hospital so quickly! Truth be told, he was already in the building visiting a sick patient, but he came over to recite a quick prayer with us. In one of the funnier moments of the day, he was about three words into a prayer when a team of four nurses and techs walked into the room, ready to wheel Jenya into the operating room. They all froze in silence and bowed their heads; it was equally amusing and respectful, and we'll never forget it.

Within a couple minutes, Jenya was off to the operating room. I was told they'd be back for me in just a bit. And so I waited, alone, again.

If your partner's pregnancy is high-risk or you've had a previous loss, push for an OB who has real experience with complicated cases. A provider who listens, explains everything, and takes your concerns seriously, can make a huge difference in how supported both of you feel.

Genetic tests and ultrasounds (like the NT scan) aren't just routine — they're tools that help catch issues early and give you peace of mind. Advocate for the most comprehensive testing available, especially if you've had a bumpy road to this pregnancy.

For older moms or high-risk pregnancies, ask your doctor about the risks of going full-term. In some cases, a planned C-section at 38 weeks may be safer than waiting. Being informed and involved in this decision shows up as real support.

Things can happen fast — like sudden bleeding or labor symptoms. Don't wait to figure it out on the fly. Know the route to the hospital, who to call, and what bags to grab. Being the calm, ready one in a crisis is one of the biggest ways you can show up.

Chapter Ten

About 15 minutes after they wheeled Jenya into the operating room, a nurse came back to get me.

"Matt, we're ready for you; Jenya's doing great in there."

We walked down a short hallway, and for the first time in my life, I was in a real-world, functioning operating room.

"Hi Matt, come on in," bellowed Dr. L. as I looked around a room with bright lights, tons of equipment, and about five masked and gowned professionals surrounding my wife on the table. There was a stool situated to the left of Jenya; I was told to have a seat. The anesthesiologist was across from me, and there was an upright sheet at my wife's waist, with doctors and others "south of the border," so to speak. It was truly fascinating; my wife was fully alert but seemed a bit out of it. The anesthesiologist told me it was completely normal. I could see Dr. L. doing some maneuvering and starting to ask for towels to mop up some of the blood that was discharging from Jenya.

Within several minutes, words that neither of us were expecting to hear came from the doctor.

"He's breech! But I've got him!"

And just like that, I went into dad mode. Like any other dad in a modern hospital, surrounded by experts who knew what they were doing, I grabbed my phone and started to take pictures. I literally stuck my arm in the air, over the sheet at Jenya's waist, and started snapping away, hoping to get a clean shot. But it was what I heard next that was truly magical – a crying baby.

"Matt, do you want to cut the cord?"

I looked over my left shoulder, and there was a gowned and masked woman standing near me, with a couple other gowned nurses flanking her. This was the NICU team that is present at every C-section at this hospital – just in case they're needed. She lowered her surgical mask and said, "Hi, it's me, Dr. LG. I wanted to be here for this." The same doctor who delivered the worst news of my life two years prior was in the room to give me some of the best news I'd ever received. I welled up, followed the trio over to the warming unit where our newborn son was being cleaned off and weighed. His cry was so boisterous, so impressive, it was music to my ears. A nurse asked Dr. LG about his APGAR score (on a scale of 0-10, this rates a newborn's health), and without hesitation, she said, "It's a 9!" I traded my cell phone for a pair of hospital scissors and ceremoniously cut the cord. A nurse asked me if we had a name for him. I didn't even have to confirm with Jenya – this boy was most-certainly, unquestionably, the name we had imagined: Samuel Giovanni Seigel.

After the nurses swaddled him up, I carried Sammy back to Jenya while the doctors were continuing to close her up. Within seconds of setting him on her chest, his little head lurched towards her breast, and he latched on like a total pro. Partners reading this, you probably know (or soon will know) that just about any mom who is interested in breastfeeding her baby treats it as an all-consuming process. There is self-imposed pressure to get it right; there are pumps, flanges, tubes, and countless other pieces of equipment to assist; and yes, there are lactation consultants, women who get paid to help other women properly breastfeed. So, not only was our baby getting some nutrition a few minutes into his life, his mother was relieved of one of the biggest post-partum stressors known to women. And for that, we were all *very* thankful!

While Sammy was nursing, there was still a lot of activity happening "on the other side of the sheet." Dr. L. and several others were busy working to close up Jenya. On a nearby cart, there was a plastic sheet with a bunch of pockets – something one might use to hold shoes in an upright position in a closet –

and they were putting blood-soaked washcloths into it. I knew they were just trying to keep track of how much blood Jenya lost throughout the C-section, but little did I know it was starting to add up.

About an hour after we were brought into a recovery room, Dr. L. came by to officially meet our baby. He said to Jenya, 'Technically, you hemorrhaged enough blood to warrant a transfusion. It's up to you if you want it – you'll probably feel better sooner, but I understand if you don't.' She didn't even blink an eye: "I'll take it!"

Dr. L. was surprised: "I had budgeted 20 minutes for this conversation," he quipped. I'll never forget him giving me a bear hug and saying with as much sincerity as I've ever heard, "Thank you for letting me deliver your baby."

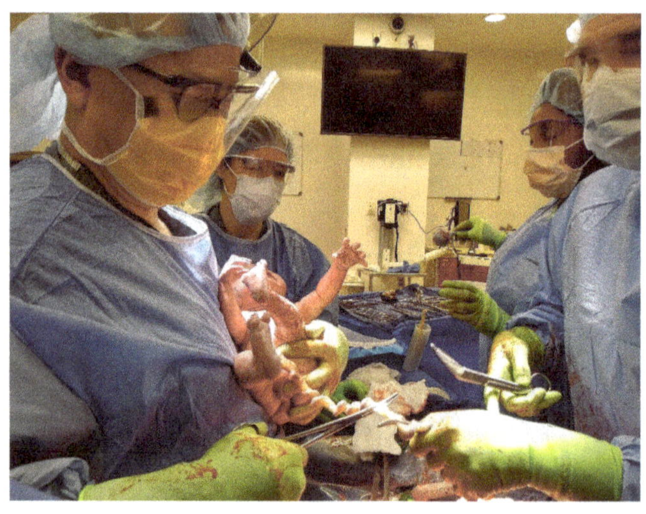

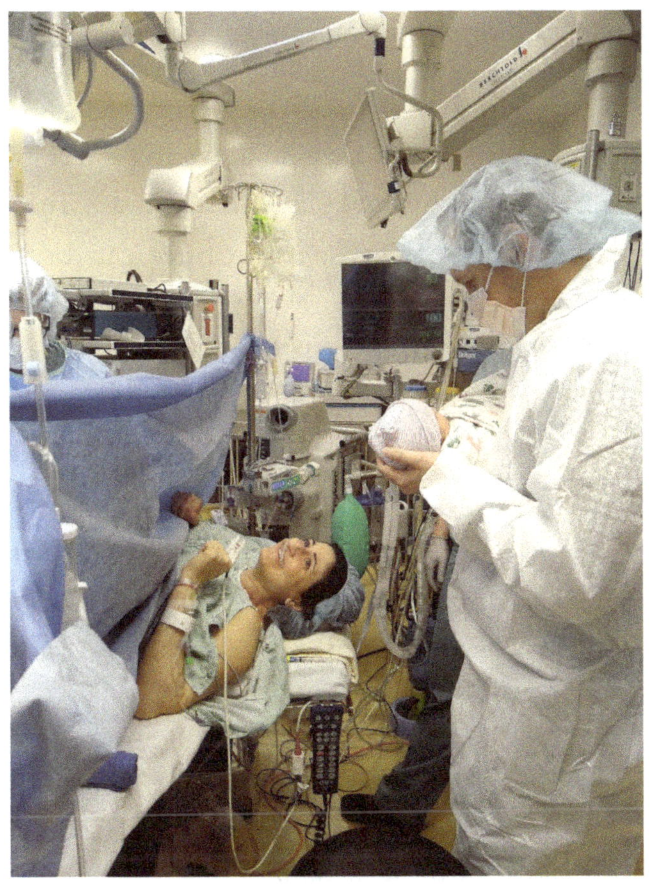

The next few days were spent in the hospital as Jenya recovered from her C-section and Samuel learned to cry and poop. I learned how to properly diaper and swaddle a baby (the nurses still do it better than I ever will). We had several visitors, including four grandparents who were beaming with pride when they got to hold their healthy grandson for the first time. The one piece of advice I received and will pass on here is that it's crucial to get as much sleep as you can in the hospital, and let the nurses help however they can, because in about 48-72 hours, they won't be there anymore!

In those first couple of days, they do a hearing screening on the baby, as well as make him take a "car seat test." This is often done with premature babies to ensure they can breathe in a reclined position. Samuel had to stay in the car seat for 90 minutes while they monitored his heart rate and breathing; he passed with flying colors.

Your baby might come out breech or there may be unexpected moments, but trust the team around you. You don't need medical training to be helpful — your calm presence, hand-holding, and camera work matter more than you think. You'll remember those first moments forever, so stay grounded, stay present.

If you're offered the chance to cut the umbilical cord, take it. It's symbolic and empowering. And when that NICU doctor who once delivered bad news shows up to celebrate your new baby? It's okay to cry. Being emotionally present doesn't make you less of a partner — it makes you a better parent.

Even after delivery, complications like hemorrhaging can happen. Ask questions and speak up if your partner looks wiped out or "off." When the doctor offers something like a transfusion, be a sounding board — and trust your partner to know what she needs. Support her decision without second-guessing.

Ask the nurses for help. Watch how they swaddle, change diapers, calm your baby. This is your "bootcamp." And don't feel guilty letting them take the baby for a bit so you can both rest. You're about to go home where it's just the two of you — and a newborn who doesn't care what time it is.

Chapter Eleven

Three days after the delivery, Jenya and I got to do something that we'd been trying to do for several years; take our baby home from the hospital. My Honda was ready for this: the car seat base was properly installed, the mirror on the headrest was affixed so we could see the baby from the front seats, and blankets were at the ready. I brought the car around to the loading zone where Jenya and Samuel were awaiting, flanked by a couple of nurses who were there to assist. We clicked the car seat into the base, closed the door, and off we went – three Seigels in one car, for the first time ever.

Children's Hospital of Wisconsin is about a half hour drive from our house, but we wanted to make a quick stop – an important stop – on our way home. After 10 minutes on the road, we brought Samuel to meet his brother at the cemetery where he rests. Benjamin is in a mausoleum, and on this beautiful May day, the sun was shining and the birds were chirping. Jenya and I each put a hand on our newborn and another hand on Benjamin's nameplate. Our family of four was together for the first time – and despite our bittersweet emotions in that moment, it was an unforgettable experience that helps to define the importance of keeping Benjamin's memory alive.

We made it home shortly thereafter and, true to form, it was feeding time. Jenya and the baby eased into our new glider in the nursery, and I unpacked the car and threw in a load of laundry. We were officially "parenting at home."

One of the things that came up in the parenting classes we took before Benjamin was a discussion about SIDS, or Sudden Infant Death Syndrome. A key contributor to helping prevent SIDS is having your baby share a bedroom with his or her parents. Not a bed, but a bedroom. So, I assembled the high-tech bassinet in our bedroom, flanking our bed. The American Academy of Pediatrics recommends having baby share a room for the first year[1]. I don't know many people who keep their babies in their bedroom that long, but we weren't going to cut things short. Bassinets come in various shapes, sizes, and price points. Fortunately for us, Jenya's cousin was kind enough to lend us his SNOO. This thing was very cool – you put your baby into what is essentially a strait jacket (or swaddle) with clips on it that connect to the mattress pad. Then, once the baby is situated,

---

1. https://www.aap.org/en/patient-care/safe-sleep/

you can turn it on – a white noise machine begins to play and the bassinet starts to gently rock your baby to sleep. There are other features, but it isn't for everyone, and it isn't cheap…and I'm not a paid spokesman for the company, so we'll leave it at that. But we did use it for about five months before transitioning Sammy into a crib, which we set up in our bedroom.

Besides the SIDS research, which is obviously reason enough to keep your newborn close by, there are plenty of other benefits for both mom and dad. If she's breastfeeding, she can grab the baby and bring him into bed to feed. At 2am, when it's feeding and diaper changing time, and you're all awake, a step saved is a win for everyone. And at 4am, if the baby starts crying, it's much easier to take a few steps to try and soothe the little guy or girl instead of sleepwalking into another room.

There does come a point when the baby will only wake up once a night to eat – and for a few weeks, it feels like the greatest gift in the world – only one interruption per night! Some babies will "sleep through the night" after a couple of months; others will take up to a year. And let's talk about that term, "sleep through the night" for a moment. If you search anywhere online, many sites will consider "sleeping through the night" to mean a six-hour stretch of sleep. Last time I checked, if you put the baby to sleep around 6 or 7pm, that means they are waking up around 2 or 3am…not exactly "through the night!" I've heard of multiple arrangements when it comes to nighttime feeding. Some moms want to do it all, some moms who aren't breastfeeding want to either take turns or alternate nights. Some partners are working long hours, others are not. There are affluent people who hire night nurses – lucky them! I can only share my experience, and that was that when Jenya was breastfeeding, she was awake. When she would pump and we'd use a bottle, I was up. When we switched to formula, we took turns. It only seemed fair to both of us. And to those of you who are working full time while helping with nighttime feedings, good on you.

The transition from bassinet to crib, and from shared room sleeping to moving your baby into his/her own room is a very personal one. In addition to the SIDS concern, there's also each family's layout of their sleeping quarters. Some parents don't want to be walking around in the middle of the night, bleary-eyed, trying to tend to their little person. Others want to see if their baby will "cry it out" as soon as they can. Again, personal choice here. The same goes for sleep training, if that's something you are considering. There are books, videos, online courses, and other tools out there to help new parents figure out the best way to have their child sleep through the night, in their own space, without waking or attempting to climb out of the crib (I've seen it happen!). There are also sleep sacks, suits, and other "gear" designed to help little ones sleep. We've used both sleeveless and "starfish" style suits that give babies a sense of containment and comfort, without being as tight as a swaddle. They also provide warmth for those of you in cold weather climates – this is important since babies shouldn't have a blanket or any other items in their crib with them for the first year.

As for the actual sleep training, we waited until about 10-12 months before we agreed that it was time. Granted, I had been pushing for us to move Samuel to his own room and sleep train him about five months prior, but I digress! Nobody likes to hear a baby cry, but if you are patient, consistent, and understanding that your child is simply communicating his or her displeasure of being alone, it's fairly easy to train your child to sleep 10-12 hours. It took my wife a good amount of restraint to not bolt into Samuel's room to pick him up, try to feed him, or do other "mom" things to comfort her child. But she was willing to follow the plan and we are both so glad she did. His sleeping habits improved within several days and we were all getting better rest, which meant we were more productive during the day and less irritable at night.

I didn't write this book to talk about the joys and challenges of raising an infant or toddler, but rather about the process of building a family. There are plenty of good reads that help with parenting in general. What Jenya and I went through to have a live, healthy child was something I don't wish upon my worst enemy. But we both have siblings, and we were determined to create a living sibling for Samuel. True to form, that would be easier said than done.

Leaving the hospital with your newborn is a moment that hits hard — a physical manifestation of your journey into fatherhood. Make sure the car seat is installed correctly (many fire stations will inspect this for free) and prepare the car ahead of time. That first ride home is filled with emotions: joy, anxiety, and in some cases, grief — and that's okay. Honor it all.

Room sharing (not bed sharing) for the first 6–12 months reduces the risk of SIDS. A bassinet in your bedroom can make nighttime feeding, soothing, and check-ins much easier — especially if your partner is breastfeeding. If you have access to a "smart" bassinet, great. If not, any firm, safe sleep surface will do. No blankets, toys, or bumpers — just baby, in a sleep sack or swaddle.

Whether you're taking shifts, doing it all together, or supporting a breastfeeding partner, communicate and collaborate. There's no universal timeline for when to move baby to their own room or how to handle sleep training — but being on the same page is key. Sleep training might involve some crying, but it doesn't make you a bad parent — it can be a step toward better rest for the whole family.

Loss after infertility and IVF is devastating — even more so when you've already been through it before. If a doctor recommends shifting your path (like exploring surrogacy), it's not a failure. It's a recognition of reality and a sign that you're still fighting for your family. As a partner, your quiet strength, open mind, and support for your partner's needs are what matter most in these moments.

Chapter Twelve

Sammy was about 20 months old when we decided we would transfer another embryo for Jenya to carry. I am three and a half years older than my brother, and Jenya is two and a half years younger than hers, so we figured this would be a good age gap for Sammy and a future sibling. The good news is that we had nine frozen embryos in storage, so we felt pretty good about having another healthy child. We did this transfer with the same fertility doctor, and everything went as expected. Of course, that meant the real anxiety would kick in – would this little fetus grow? We went back to the clinic for a six-week ultrasound, and the heartbeat was strong! We were officially discharged from the clinic and released to Dr. L., our OB, back in Milwaukee.

We were scheduled for a 12-week ultrasound on Monday morning, July 5, 2021. It was the end of the long holiday weekend, and my parents were able to hang out with Sammy while we went for the routine exam. It was a quiet day at the hospital and we were able to easily park and make our way to the maternal fetal medicine wing. An ultrasound technician took us to the room, Jenya got on the table, and the technician inserted the probe to begin the ultrasound. We saw a head, and a body, and within a second, Jenya said, "I can't believe it. How could this possibly happen again?"

There was no heartbeat.

The tech had no answer. Dr. L., who happened to be on call that morning, came to visit with us, equally befuddled by the whole thing. What he said next would solidify our plan to complete our family.

"Jenya, you've been through a lot. There is a great deal of scar tissue in your uterus, I saw it the last time we did a D&C. I really think surrogacy is the best way to go at this point."

"Then that's what we'll do," she responded. I nodded in agreement – quite frankly, I had been leaning that way before we tried this most-recent transfer with Jenya, but she wanted to give it another shot, and I was willing to support her choice. So just like that, Jenya's road to becoming pregnant with our third child came to a screeching halt. This was devastating for her, and I felt terrible knowing that she felt as if she had failed…even though that was hardly the case. She had my unconditional support to find the right person to carry our next baby, and I made sure she knew we'd take as much time as we needed to find the right match.

Family, friends, clergy, and others were happy to connect us with others who have turned to gestational carriers to build their family – otherwise known as surrogates. There are two main ways to find a surrogate: you either know someone willing to carry a baby for you, or you hire an agency to help you find a carrier. After speaking with others who had been through the process, we decided that we'd interview agencies while also looking on our own. It turns out, our fertility clinic requires prospective parents to use an agency. I don't know if that's the case everywhere, but it was the policy where we had our embryos stored.

We met virtually with a few surrogacy agencies. They were all professional, some were a bit more "slick" than others with their marketing materials, but they all had one thing in common – they weren't cheap! This was going to be an expensive proposition – think "college tuition" expensive – but we had been saving a lot of our income, not going on vacations, and been relatively frugal ever since we started the process with Sammy; this wasn't an impossibility for us. I know that many, many people can't afford to go down this path and it's heartbreaking, especially for people of limited means who truly want to grow their family. I know I'm also fortunate to have an employer that provides an adoption & surrogacy benefit – in my case, it was $25,000 towards the cost.

After Jenya and I weighed the pros and cons of each agency, we decided to move forward with one that was not "all-inclusive" but rather allowed us to use an attorney of our choosing (they provided referrals) and kind of piece-meal together our surrogacy plan. They told us they were confident they'd match us with a carrier within 12-14 weeks of signing a contract with them. So, we signed, filled out a ton of paperwork, and did a virtual interview with our intake specialist. She wanted to get to know the two of us; our preferences for a surrogate (was she within driving distance, did she have a COVID vaccination, was she married, did she live in a surrogate-friendly state), and our "deal-breakers." Then it was time for us to wait for some good news. Each week, we'd get an email from the specialist, telling us they were working hard to find someone for us. One week turned into two, two into four, and so on…and we weren't getting any matches. We didn't think we were *that* picky – we preferred someone in the Midwest who had been vaccinated for COVID (we started this journey during the summer of 2021). There was some fresh research out that a pregnant woman with COVID was likely to have complications with childbirth[1]. I don't know if that is still the case, but obviously, there was a lot of information (and misinformation) during that oh-so-memorable time of our lives. We were getting a little antsy…and a little frustrated.

While the agency was allegedly looking for a match for us, our

---

1. https://www.acog.org/womens-health/faqs/coronavirus-covid-19-pregnancy-and-breastfeeding

personal network was also on the hunt. About 12 weeks after we had hired the agency, one of Jenya's friend's friends said she knew someone in Chicago who wanted to be a gestational carrier for a family in need. Jenya immediately got in contact with her. We set up a virtual meeting, learned about her family, her two adorable boys, and her "why." The feeling was right for all of us and we were ready to move forward with her! Now we had to have a conversation with our agency – because there was no way we were going to pay them thousands of dollars for not holding up their end of the deal. If it was up to me, we would have fired them, but our fertility clinic required intended parents like us to have an agency and we had a signed contract with the agency. Some of these organizations are in cahoots, I swear! The agency ended up cutting their fee in half (saving us about $10,000).

Now that we had a surrogate and an agency, we had to hire a lawyer to draw up the contract between the surrogate and us. Each state has different laws; some states are surrogate friendly while others don't permit it at all. It's important to remember that the state in which the child is born is what matters, not the state in which you live. Illinois happens to be a very friendly state when it comes to surrogacy, and we were introduced to a lawyer in Chicago who was amazing. You may have noticed I haven't mentioned any other providers by their full name – but Ryan Ferrante will go down as one of the most professional, responsive, and easygoing people I've ever worked with. Maybe it's because he's been through the surrogacy journey himself, or maybe it's because he's just a good guy, but I cannot recommend him enough if you are ever in my shoes.

What I found very interesting about the process is that we also had to pay for a *different* attorney for our surrogate. The agency provided her with a couple of options, and she selected one, who Ryan had extensive experience with. Most of the contract is pretty standard, however there were a few items for which we had to negotiate. Was the surrogate allowed to leave the state? If so, up to what point in the pregnancy? How many days off were we willing to pay for her husband to attend doctors' appointments and postpartum? There are a lot of things that we certainly didn't think about heading into this process, and having a reputable attorney draft a fair contract is a key to a successful experience for everyone involved.

Once the ink was dry, it was time to schedule an embryo transfer. Our fertility doctor's office made those arrangements; we made the all-too-familiar drive to that office and met our gestational carrier and her husband in person for the first time. We hit it off right away, and the transfer went as you'd expect. It was a little more crowded in the procedure room; our surrogate was kind enough to invite Jenya and me to join her and her husband during the transfer. The four of us said a quick prayer, hoping this embryo would stick and grow, and we went our separate ways, knowing we'd be seeing each other sooner than later.

We would get weekly "check in" emails from our case manager which, quite frankly, were worthless to us. Jenya and our carrier were texting nearly every day, and everything was moving along just fine. We drove to Chicagoland for the 20-week ultrasound, took a tour of the hospital where the delivery was scheduled to occur, and had a wonderful brunch before heading back to Milwaukee. After all of the heartache we had experienced at previous ultrasounds, it was a massive relief for both of us to know that there was a healthy boy growing inside of our hero, our surrogate.

Around 28 weeks, we made arrangements for Sammy, who was about three and a half, to meet the "helper" who was carrying our next child. We spent a Saturday driving down to Chicagoland, where Sammy met the helper (and her noticeable belly!), along with her husband and two sons. The kids hit it off beautifully; we had a lively lunch as a group of seven (plus baby in utero), the boys played with a LOT of toys, and Sammy was able to feel his baby brother kicking around for a bit. It was perfect.

If you're an expectant, married person reading this, you've likely experienced a time when your partner started to act like someone you didn't marry. Maybe she was extra needy, extra whiny, extra moody. Maybe she was just certifiably crazy for a bit! Just wait until the third trimester, when she's getting larger and rounder. Those "her-mones" during pregnancy are extra special. I can't even imagine how it was going in our surrogate's house – for her, her husband, and her two young kids. It's one thing to decide that you want to help another family by carrying their baby; it's next-level to do it while having to explain to your two kids – both under age 5 – that the baby in her belly is going to go to another family. We are forever grateful to our "helper" and her family, and we still keep in touch to this day.

Our carrier's two previous deliveries went quickly and smoothly. We were excited about the prospects of a normal birth. Our plan to have Sammy sleep over at his godparents' house had been established and their two older sons were ready for our three-year-old to invade their space for a couple of days.

On March 15, 2023, Jenya woke me up in the middle of the night.

"Hey babe, wake up, it's time."

"Huh?" I said, still half asleep.

"She just called. Her water broke, it's time to go."

And just like that, it was all systems go – four weeks early! We had to pack our overnight bags and quickly shower and load the car. I installed a rear-facing car seat and base while scarfing down a banana. Jenya woke Sammy from a deep sleep. He didn't complain one bit – possibly because he was half asleep, probably because he was excited to meet his brother. We hopped in the car and drove the eight minutes to our friends, Sammy's godparents' house. As we pulled into the driveway, Jenya called, and nobody answered the phone. She called again while I got out of the car and rang their doorbell, to which nobody was answering. Were they not home? It was four in the morning – they must be! I was banging on the door for a good five minutes when their dog finally started barking. Then, Sammy's godmother carried Sammy inside as her eight-year-old son came running downstairs, exclaiming "It's the sleepover!" The nervous, excited energy was palpable, but Sammy was in the best hands as Jenya and I rolled out to make the two-hour drive south.

Traffic at that hour was light, and we arrived at the hospital around 6am. After checking in, receiving our ID bracelets, and working through some logistics (as the intended parents, but with Jenya not the one in labor, you sometimes have a little extra explaining to do as this isn't an everyday thing for the hospital workers), Jenya was allowed to go to the surrogate's room. In the post-COVID world, they established a one visitor policy, so I was relegated to the waiting room until we were given a room for ourselves. I scouted out the cafeteria, grabbed Jenya a coffee, and opened my laptop to get caught up on a little work. Word was, despite her water breaking, she was only four centimeters dilated. There were several people in the waiting room, mostly the age of grandparents…so many of them were looking at me with a great deal of skepticism, thinking "why is he not in there with his wife?" I had a nice conversation with four grandparents that had just met their first grandson, one at a time. It was actually pretty neat to be in this spot; I was planning to end the day with a newborn in my arms, and I got to witness the joy many other parents and grandparents were experiencing, some for the first time.

Our surrogate's dilation and labor was a long, slow process, very similar to what Jenya and I experienced with Benjamin. Despite her water having broken at 4am, she was only 4-5 centimeters dilated by mid-day. They gave her a very low dose of Pitocin, which was only administered when the OB was able to supervise her. Just how slow were things going? I brought my work laptop with me to the hospital as March is a busy time of year in my professional life. We had a quarterly corporate conference call scheduled at 2pm that day, and I was on it. In front of about 40 others, my Vice President of Sales exclaimed, "We know you all know how important these calls are, and we appreciate you making time for them. I mean, Matt's about to have a baby and he's here!" We all got a chuckle, and I still have that chip to cash in if I need to.

I left the hospital to grab Jenya and myself a pizza for dinner. During that time, our surrogate received an epidural as her pain was starting to increase. Despite having injected Jenya hundreds of times with IVF medications, and having taken plenty of flu, COVID, and other vaccines throughout my life, the visual of seeing an anesthesiologist jam a large needle into a woman's back is not something I enjoy; I'm glad I wasn't there when that happened. Jenya and I ate dinner in a room down the hallway from where our surrogate was in labor. The room adjacent to the surrogate's was going to be opening up the following day, so we didn't fully unpack our bags. After what felt like an eternity, the OB showed up around 8pm and the Pitocin was turned back on. At 10:30pm, her cervix was dilated to 7.5 centimeters – we were getting there, slowly but surely.

It turned out to be a pretty busy night in the labor and delivery ward. The OB was busy handling a few other deliveries, and the nurse assigned to us was helping the surrogate as her labor progressed. Labor and delivery nurses truly are the unsung heroes of childbirth. They are there from start to finish, and while it's the doctor making the final call on almost every medical decision, the nurses are the coaches, the pain managers, and the conduit between patient and provider. I made it a point to let every nurse we came across know how much we appreciate them – they've got a tough gig and are totally underappreciated. Next time you're in the hospital for any reason, be sure to be nice to your nurses!

Around 1am, the epidural began to wear off, and our surrogate was starting to feel a good amount of pressure and pain. She asked us to call her husband and see if he could come back to the hospital – they both thought this baby was going to be out of her a long while ago, just like her first two deliveries went with her own kids! He was able to return to the hospital within 45 minutes to be by her side. The nurses were having her push while she was 9 or 9.5 centimeters dilated. But the baby wasn't moving down the birth canal. Obviously, I cannot judge another person's pain tolerance, but I had never seen another person appear to be in so much agony – I felt terrible. Finally, shortly before 3am, the OB said to our surrogate, "It's time to make a decision." But he didn't provide any options! My goodness, you have a woman who has never had (and didn't prefer) a C-section, a married couple who desperately want a healthy child, and a doctor who's clearly tired and disengaged, and therefore not providing much in the way of medical advice. Here's how the next 90 seconds went:

Doctor: "Well, we could do a vacuum while you push."

Surrogate: "Oh my, I know they are so dangerous, but I really don't…"

Jenya and I looked at each other, flashing back to our first delivery with Benjamin. I knew exactly what she was about to say next.

Jenya: "Isn't it true that if the vacuum fails you are going to progress to a C-section, so it would actually potentially be faster to go directly to a C-section?"

Doctor: "Yes, that is true."

Surrogate (while crying in pain): "I really wanted to deliver vaginally."

Me: "(Surrogate), there is no shame in a C-section, you don't need to be a hero."

Surrogate: "Let's do the C-section."

Doctor, to nurse: "All right, let's prep the O.R."

Now, there was a bit of urgency here. Our surrogate was in pain, the baby was stuck in the birth canal, and Jenya and I were quickly going to a dark place, with memories of a botched delivery six years prior at the forefront of our minds. That said, Jenya and I are positive that if it hadn't been for our previous experience, we wouldn't have known about all of our options and Jenya certainly wouldn't have spoken up the way she did. They eventually wheeled the surrogate away to the operating room, and her husband put on scrubs before the three of us walked down the hallway to a nursery area just across a corridor from the operating room. We were doing our best to assure her husband that she was going to be fine. This wasn't nearly as emergent as our C-section with Benjamin, but it was still quite uncomfortable, especially for someone that had never been in this position before. While it felt like an eternity, a nurse came to get him after about 10 minutes – we told him to come back with good news.

Jenya and I were alone in the room, and she was starting to get upset – understandably. Last time I was alone in a room like this, it was with a doula, and I was exceptionally scared. This time I was alone with Jenya and now I had some experience to lean on. I did my best to reassure her that things were going to be fine. This was "urgent," not "emergent," I told her. Additionally, there wasn't nearly as much chaos this time around…which was 1000% true. After a few minutes, a nurse came in and told us things were proceeding just fine, and that unfortunately, this happens quite often. Jenya and I said a short prayer and waited in silence for a few more minutes until the surrogate's husband came back, tears in his eyes.

"She's OK…and the baby is beautiful," he exclaimed while giving us both a giant hug! The sense of relief I felt was unlike anything I'd felt before, and in no time at all, the nurse came into a room with a little bundle of joy for us to meet.

Ari Carmelo Seigel was actually sunny side up in the birth canal and a little blue. They had to give him oxygen for a minute – his one-minute Apgar score was 7 – but he quickly recovered, crying the sweet cry that every baby makes. At 6 lb, 5 oz, he was good-sized for a preemie. The nurses cleaned him up, swaddled him, and we were headed back to our room in the wee hours of the morning, newborn in tow. The next morning, I went downstairs and grabbed coffee for Jenya and our surrogate, who was in the adjacent room, while the pediatrician came in for a quick check-up. We elected to have Ari circumcised in the hospital; when Jenya asked the doctor whether she used a Plastibell or a clamp (the two main tools used in circumcision), she responded, without hesitation, that she uses a Plastibell because "it produces a better aesthetic outcome." This line will go down as one of the funniest things I've ever heard in a medical setting in my life.

Being the old pro that I was, I was more than happy to help change one of Ari's first diapers in the hospital. We took some newborn pictures, spent time connecting with family via FaceTime, and Jenya spoke with a feeding specialist as she was going to try to nurse despite not having carried the baby. (Yes, there are pills that can be taken to induce lactation) We spent more time with our surrogate and her husband; the best news of the day was that everyone was going home the next morning. That two-hour drive home was a lot different than the 30-

minute drive I made with Sammy in the back seat. For one, Jenya and I stopped at a drive-through window to grab some lunch shortly after we left the hospital! There were far fewer nerves this time around, and we were equally excited to introduce Ari to his big brother, who was waiting at our house with his godmother.

Walking into our house, baby carrier in hand, big brother sprinting to get a look at his new sibling, will go down as a top five moment in my life. The pure joy I saw on Sammy's face in that instant felt incredible. I have no recollection of my parents introducing me to my younger brother (the age gap is nearly identical, a little more than 3.5 years) but the picture I have on my desktop computer of Sammy holding his brother in his lap is something I cherish every day. After years of heartache, tragedy, and perseverance, we were about to spend our first night together as a complete family: four of us on earth, and one of us in heaven. Despite that permanent hole in our hearts, Jenya and I knew that our family was as complete as it was going to be. We slept as well as parents of a three-day-old and three-year-old could and woke up the following morning, ready for a new routine: one with limited naps and no "handing off" an only child so one parent could get a break.

After about 24 hours, Sammy made it very clear he was no longer interested in being a big brother since he was no longer getting all of our attention. Jenya is a younger sibling and I'm an older one; we never really planned for how we were going to give Sammy some "special attention," but this was quickly becoming a priority for us. Our efforts to keep things as calm and serene as possible for the baby meant that we'd have to spoil Sammy a bit. We couldn't force him to spend every waking moment at home with his brother, so we planned for some one-on-one trips to the store, museum, playdates, and more to make him feel just as special. Despite our efforts, there was a moment somewhere in the first couple of months when Sammy told us to "throw the baby in the garbage!" If he only knew what we went through to bring both him and Ari into this world.

Some fertility clinics require using a surrogacy agency—check early to avoid surprises. Surrogacy typically costs a six-figure sum of money.

Legal protections vary by birth state, not your home state—choose wisely. You may have to travel a significant distance to meet your baby.

Surrogacy contracts must cover travel, appointments, and postpartum terms; a good lawyer will have everything buttoned up so that there are no conflicts down the road.

If you're fortunate to be in the delivery room and something feels off medically (e.g., stalled labor), ask direct questions and advocate for safe options. You are a vital part of the team!

Epilogue

I wrote this book to give men and women a glimpse into one family's reality when it came to fertility. You can read all the statistics and learn about all the hardship we and other couples have faced, but until you've experienced it, it truly is hard to fathom. It's taken me a long time to finish this project, probably because I was trying to think about the best way to end the story. This is a book about family building. For many, it would only require one or two chapters. Simple pregnancies, no complications, two healthy kids, and away they go with the rest of their lives. But for many others, a lengthy story is in the cards. Like so many other facets of life, you don't get to know ahead of time how long your story is going to be until you are finished building your family. It took us more than six years to have our three boys, two of whom are alive today. In retrospect, it's not an exorbitant length of time. But when you are in it, dealing with tragedy, heartbreak, and emotions (your own and those of your partner), not to mention the financial implications of each decision, the mental toll it takes can be overwhelming. Hit a wall and bad things can happen to your relationship. Be kind to yourself and your partner and love will persevere. Jenya and I chose the latter and our family is eternally better for it.

Acknowledgments

This book wouldn't have been possible without the loving support of my wife, Jenya, my parents, Sandi and Warren, and my brother, Scott. Thank you for being coaches, sounding boards, and confidants.

To all of the health care workers – the doctors, nurses, NICU therapists and technicians, support staff and mental health experts – thank you.

To our 'helper,' her husband and two amazing boys – thank you. Ari wouldn't be here without you.

To Dana, Don, Lara, Todd, and Bette, whose feedback and perspective were instrumental in wrapping up this project – thank you.

To all of the men and women who are desperately trying to start, grow, and/or finish their family – I see you. Thank you for reading.

About the Author

Matt Seigel is a husband, father, and television advertising executive whose first career was spent as a sports anchor and reporter. Writing *Not How I Drew It Up* — his debut book — allowed him to return to his journalism roots while sharing a deeply personal story. Matt and his family are committed to openness about fertility struggles, hoping their journey encourages others to find strength, support, and honest conversation along the way. When he's not chasing his boys around, he's chasing errant golf shots.